Stickin' to the Union

Stickin' to the Union

Local 2224 vs. John Buhler

Doug Smith

Fernwood Publishing • Halifax, Nova Scotia

Editing: Robert Clarke
Cover design: Rob Niedzwiecki, Doowah Design Inc.
Printed and bound in Canada by:
University of Toronto Press Inc.

A publication of:
Fernwood Publishing
32 Oceanvista Lane, Site 2A, Box 5,
Black Point, Nova Scotia, B0J 1B0
and 324 Clare Avenue
Winnipeg, Manitoba, R3L 1S3
www.fernwoodbooks.ca

Fernwood Publishing Company Limited gratefully acknowledges
the financial support of the Department of Canadian Heritage,
the Nova Scotia Department of Tourism and Culture
and the Canada Council for the Arts for our publishing program.

Library and Archives Canada Cataloguing in Publication
Smith, Doug, 1954-
Stickin' to the union: Local 224 vs. John Buhler / Doug Smith.

ISBN 1-55266-141-5

1. Versatile Industries Strike, Winnipeg, Man., 2001.
2. CAW-Canada.
Local 2224—History. I. Title. II. Title: Sticking to the union.

HD5329.M22 2001 S65 2004   331.892'8292252'09712743   C2004-903470-7

Contents

You can't scare me, I'm stickin' to the union
— Woody Guthrie

Acknowledgements

This book, commissioned by Canadian Auto Workers Local 2224, tells the story of the Local and its historic conflict with Buhler Versatile in 2000–2001. I would particularly like to thank Scott McLaren and Dale Paterson of the CAW for their trust and co-operation throughout this project.

In writing this book I spoke with more than a score of former Versatile workers: they set aside considerable amounts of time to speak openly about an event that was often painful to discuss: I remain eternally grateful to them for their generosity. A number of former members declined to be interviewed, particularly those who had been involved in the Hydraulic Engineering Workers Association, the predecessor to the CAW at Versatile. To the best of my abilities I have tried to present a fair rendering of the views of those former Versatile workers who did agree to be interviewed. While members of Local 2224 read the manuscript and commented on my misinterpretations of fact, they also provided me with the freedom to tell this story as I saw fit.

I also interviewed other people who were involved in the conflict, including Garth Smorang and Gary Doer, and individuals who were involved in the Local's early struggles, including Barrie Farrow, Hemi Mitic, and Mel Myers. I appreciate the time that all these individuals gave me, and their co-operation. Nolan Reilly, John Loxley, Wayne Antony, Dennis Lewycky, and Tom Langford also read and commented on the manuscript—I am grateful for their advice and assistance. Thanks as well to the production folk at Fernwood Publishing: Debbie Mathers, Beverley Rach, and Tim Dunn; also thanks to Robert Clarke for copyediting and Rob Niedzwiecki at Doowah Design for the cover.

While I can understand their reluctance to become involved in this project, I regret that both John Buhler and Craig Engel declined my requests to be interviewed.

1

"You're Not Getting a Dime"

As they sat in the union boardroom on September 29, 2000, waiting for the arrival of the company representatives, the members of Canadian Auto Workers (CAW) Local 2224 bargaining team were far from certain of what they could expect. The Local had represented the workers at the Versatile tractor plant in south Winnipeg for fifteen years, but the meeting that Friday marked the first day of bargaining with the company's new owner.

Some four months earlier John Buhler, a local entrepreneur, had bought the Versatile tractor plant. For over a decade the plant had been owned by one large corporation or another—Cornat, Ford, and Fiat had all had a piece of the plant since 1987. There was always a danger that a plant in Winnipeg on the bald Canadian prairies might get lost in the multinational shuffle, but in the modern tractor business being owned by a global corporation had considerable advantages. When Ford New Holland owned the Versatile plant, the tractors turned out in south Winnipeg were marketed all over the world by the corporation's network of 6,000 dealers.

All of the global tractor manufacturers were used to dealing with unions—even if they often dealt with them roughly. They all had labour relations departments and standardized and professional approaches to bargaining. They might be prepared to see how far they could make a union bend, but it was not their policy to break a union.

The bargaining team was less certain about John Buhler's intentions. The members knew of his reputation as an eccentric, a bottom-feeder, and a turnaround artist whose disparate empire included an agricultural implements division, a furniture company, a glassworks, and a lumberyard. A few years earlier Buhler and the CAW had clashed at Greensteel Industries, a small metal-manufacturing plant in Winnipeg—and in that case Buhler had succeeded in driving the union out. The CAW was not out for revenge, but the union had made it clear that Buhler was just about the last person it wanted to see take over the plant from Fiat in the spring of 2000. Some of the employees feared that he was buying the plant simply to shut it down, while others worried that he intended to drastically reduce the workforce by contracting out as much work as possible (some of it, perhaps, to other Buhler-owned companies). All of them expected that Buhler was going to be seeking major concessions from the union. Ever since they joined the CAW in 1985, Versatile workers had seen their wages and benefits improve with each contract. The message that the workers gave their bargaining team in 2000 was that they were not prepared to take any steps backward.

Dale Paterson, the senior staff CAW representative in Winnipeg, had counselled the Local to take a cautious approach. At first Paterson had considered putting a charge under the bargaining team—giving them "a blast" in front of the membership to get them moving. Thinking twice about that, instead he told the team that they would have to be "a lot smarter" than usual in these negotiations. The union couldn't do its usual "go in 'bang, bang, bang, you know, take you out on strike, you know we'll hold you out for ransom' kind of a thing." At that point, Paterson said later, he just didn't know how to do it smarter. But if nothing else, doing things smarter meant that Paterson and Scott McLaren, the chairperson of the Local's plant committee, were going to take detailed notes on everything that was said at the bargaining table.

McLaren, a veteran of numerous internal union battles, realized that the union would not make any progress without a struggle.

The very location of the bargaining session—in the union offices, in a nondescript two-storey building in south Winnipeg rather than in a hotel meeting room—was a testament to Buhler's legendary unwillingness to overpay for anything. Buhler had wanted to hold the talks at the plant, a few minutes' drive to the south of the union office in an industrial park. Like most unions, the CAW was reluctant to hold talks on company property. Holding talks on neutral territory reduced the risk of misinformation or rumours being leaked to the members as the talks proceeded. But there was no way that Buhler was prepared to pay for a hotel meeting room when he had a perfectly acceptable boardroom at his factory. In the end he agreed to meet the CAW team at the union office, so there they were, waiting for Buhler and his bargaining team.

When the elevator opened, the CAW team, which included McLaren, Paterson, and eight other members of the Local, got their next surprise. The only person who walked out was John Buhler. He was going to conduct negotiations on his own—without even having anyone there to take notes for him.

The sixty-seven-year-old Buhler hardly looked the part of a tycoon or a bully. That morning he was bubbling with excitement. He had, he said, some important news to share with the bargaining team. McLaren asked if Buhler was going to announce that he had found a distribution network, since without a string of distributors the plant had no long-term future. No, Buhler said, it was nothing like that. He just wanted to let them know that he now had $66 million in the bank. After offering to show the team his bank account—and noting that it was actually his wife's account—he repeated the $66-million figure and opened negotiations by telling the union bargaining team, "You're not getting a dime."

While the CAW bargaining team was trying to figure out if Buhler was kidding or not, the $66-million man explained that he had forgotten to bring either a pen or a pad of paper with him. Paterson gave Buhler a pen and paper. He told the owner that the union was not looking for a fight. With the conflict at Greensteel in mind, Paterson said that while the union had some history with Buhler he did not intend to let those experiences colour these negotiations. Paterson was trying to prevent the talks from getting too rancorous, but Buhler brushed aside the olive branch. He looked at the bargaining team and announced, "You're not going to like my proposals."

Before Buhler presented his proposals, McLaren outlined the CAW's opening position. As each item was introduced, Buhler in turn provided a colour commentary on the likelihood—or unlikelihood—of it being adopted. To a proposal that the bargaining unit be expanded, Buhler said he would have to be six feet under before that happened. In response to a proposal for language that would tighten the prohibitions on management personnel doing the work of union members, the owner said, "I'd propose to loosen it rather than tighten it. You don't run the factory. I run the factory." At another point he said that it ought to be possible to cut the size of the contract in half by making it much simpler. When McLaren proposed that the company would provide each worker with twelve hours of health and safety training, Buhler said, "You can't expect me to pay for it unless you take it out of the pot." The idea of a full-time health and safety representative was greeted with, "I'm not going to respond to that. You will hate my guts." Rather than accept the union proposal to ban further contracting out of work, Buhler said, "Your work will be contracted out to some union and non-union places."

Perhaps in recognition of the negative nature of what he had said so far, Buhler prefaced his own comments with a bit of a pep talk. "I wanted to build tractors since I was sixteen, now I'm sixty-seven and passionate. I can save this factory.... I've never owned a suit over $200. Let's do this together. This part isn't fun, but work should be fun." He followed up with a warning that if he were backed into a corner he would padlock the doors.

While the CAW proposals had been presented in detail, all Buhler had to offer was a single page that he said he had typed up earlier that day. (He even managed to get the union's name wrong, referring to it as the UAW rather than the CAW.) At the outset he said that he planned to increase sales by improving quality and lowering costs. He had already commenced this campaign, he said, by reducing administrative costs by 30 per cent. Buhler was proposing a two-year wage freeze, although there would be bonuses to a maximum of $1,000 a year based on the number of hours an employee worked. As Buhler went down his list, the bargaining team members came to realize that a wage freeze was one of the more palatable elements in Buhler's contract offer.

Several of Buhler's proposals focused on discouraging worker participation in the union. The most severe was a refusal to countenance the idea of a full-time union plant committee chairperson. It was common in the CAW to have the union's plant chairperson paid full-time wages by the employer to work full-time for the union, making sure the contract was being adhered to. This idea was anathema to Buhler. He turned to McLaren, the current plant committee chairperson, and said, "Sorry Scott, you're out of a job."

Buhler also announced that vacation pay would only be accumulated on the basis of hours worked—members who took leave to participate in union activity would see their vacations shortened. The company would also stop making deductions on the union's behalf to its political education fund. "If you want to collect for your social club"—Buhler's dismissive term for the union—"you do it." Nor would the employer be making contributions to the labour movement's occupational health centre. All grievances had to be settled, without arbitration, before a new contract would be agreed to. Gathering steam, Buhler explained there would be no more union offices in the plant, and if employees were going to file grievances the matters would all be handled after regular business hours. He also thought the union did not need such a large bargaining committee.

The number of paid holidays was to be reduced from fifteen to ten days. The payout in life insurance was to be reduced from $40,000 to $25,000, and for accidental death and disability from $80,000 to $50,000. In every past contract the CAW had managed to negotiate improvements to the pension plan. When the CAW was certified at the plant in 1985 the pension plan paid out $10 a month for each year of service. By 2000 it was paying out $34 a month for each year of service. Buhler was not prepared to negotiate any further improvements in the plan. A freeze in the increase in pension benefits would have a dramatic impact on the membership's retirement incomes.

But there was more: the three biggest proposed changes involved the benefit plan, seniority, and limits on contracting out. Buhler said he intended on bringing in the Buhler Versatile Health and Dental Benefits Plan, the same plan that he provided at the other plants he owned. As he described it, the plan would provide each worker with up to $1,000 a year to spend on medical benefits. Unspent money could be carried over to the next year and used to buy shares in the company. Buhler wanted to reduce the maximum amount to be paid to workers on long-term disability from $2,600 to $1,500 a month. He wanted to reduce the short-term disability benefit to no more than a worker could receive from Employment Insurance.

This was a truly aggressive proposal. The CAW's health benefit plans at Versatile was a jewel of the contract. Members paid only thirty-five cents for each drug prescription; every member of a worker's family was eligible for $150 worth of eyeglasses plus one eye examination every two years and $550 worth of hearing aid services every three years. The plan also covered hospital, ambulance, tests, and a range of other services. In total the existing plan was worth $700,000 per year more than Buhler's plan.

On the issue of seniority Buhler said he wanted to resolve questions around his ability to transfer employees within the plant. The bargaining team feared that this meant Buhler wanted to be able to pick and choose which employees would do what and which employees would be laid off. As the talks proceeded, Buhler was to make his hostility to seniority ever more apparent.

Finally, without an end to the current restrictions on outsourcing, Buhler said, the plant had no future. He wanted to delete a provision that said Versatile could not lay people off due to outsourcing. From the union's perspective, that provision had proven ineffective because management had simply contracted out work, often to Buhler Industries, and then several weeks later laid people off on the grounds that there had been a reduction in demand. The workers had wanted the provision strengthened, not eliminated.

Buhler's bravura performance left many of the bargaining team members stunned. Paul Lussier recalled a previous set of talks in which, as a joke Paterson had opened the talks by deadpanning, "This union views bargaining as a process of give and take. You are going to give and we are going to take." According to Lussier, "Dale said that in jest and it was funny." Now it "was John Buhler's attitude, and he was very serious."

Before the meeting broke up, Local 2224 president Len Rausch came up with a novel alternative to Buhler's proposals. He pointed out that in many ways the CAW contract still lagged behind the contracts the United Auto Workers had negotiated for agricultural implement workers with the John Deere company in the United States. If Buhler was up to it, Rausch said the union might even be prepared to give up its current contract in favour of a 1979 John Deere contract. Buhler was not interested. He chose to leave them with the warning that his first offer was always his best offer. He meant it.

After the owner's departure, and with those words of warning ringing in their ears, the Local 2224 bargaining team tried to make sense of what had just happened. They could not understand why Buhler had not brought anyone along to support him or take notes. Where were long-time Versatile managers Hugh Bagnall and Ken Kidd? Later on Scott McLaren recalled, "If they had been there, I think we could have reached a resolution on the issues. They were tough negotiators, but they knew the history of the plant, the way the union and company operated." By not bringing them Buhler was signalling that past practices were just that: things of the past that he was not prepared to be bound by. "He didn't want to have that relationship," McLaren said. "He didn't want that to continue on." And why was he putting so many contentious issues on the table at once? According to McLaren, "Unlimited subcontracting on its own would have been enough to trigger a strike." For Lussier the union was "headed down a very slippery path at that point in time. We knew that the wheels could fall off this cart right away, if they hadn't already."

An irresistible force and an immovable object were on a collision course. Less than a month later the Local 2224 members walked off the job. Despite warnings from McLaren that the strike would probably last for months, many of the workers believed that the strike would be over in a matter of weeks. It would be nine months before the picket lines came down, and when they did the workers had no jobs to return to. The length and bitterness of the Versatile strike were predictable. No one could have foreseen Buhler announcing that, even though the Canadian government had loaned him over $30 million to buy what was the last tractor plant in Canada, he intended to shutter the plant and reopen it in North Dakota. No one could have predicted that the CAW would be lobbying the Manitoba government to buy the plant. The union's decision to vote to return to work in the spring without a contract, the Manitoba Labour Board decision that Buhler had to pay the union $6 million in lost wages as compensation for his bargaining in bad faith, and Buhler's end-game proposal to pay the union and its members close to $20 million to go away were all bolts from the blue, all of them unprecedented.

To some observers the Versatile strike was little more than a labour relations version of the battle of the monster trucks. Indeed, as the strike neared its final days one reporter concluded that Buhler and the union deserved one another. Like all large-scale industrial disputes, this one saw plenty of posturing and bluster on both sides, but the strike also brought a series of broader questions into focus. Why are Canadians so bereft of industrial strategies that a canny entrepreneur can buffalo the federal government into virtually giving him a tractor plant? How has it come to pass that the future of a tractor designed and developed in Winnipeg was decided in Rome, Amsterdam, London, and eventually Washington? What are the limits within which a labour-friendly provincial government can operate these days?

Finally—and this is a question more rarely asked—what resources did the Versatile strikers draw upon to sustain themselves for nine months, as they saw their pasts and their futures being taken from them? Why did they not give in, give up, or go away?

Although the union won a number of stunning victories along the way, this is not a story with a happy ending. Over 250 men, all of them with at least twenty years of experience, lost their jobs. Few of them would find jobs that paid as well as the ones they had at Versatile. Not surprisingly, most of them would prefer to be still working at Versatile, but of the two dozen or so former Versatile employees that I spoke to, none had any regrets about what they did, and none wanted to have John Buhler dictating their working conditions. Every man on strike had worked at the plant before the CAW was brought in; they remembered the days when the foremen could promote favourites and lay off older workers at will. The CAW had not only provided them with better wages, better benefits, and better working conditions, but had also provided them with a collective sense of self-worth. The union and the contract were theirs, something that they had created, fought for, and defended.

To know who these men are, to know the history of their local—to examine the experiences that created a deep pool of solidarity that would nourish them for nine months—is to come to an understanding of why these workers were able to hang in for so long, an understanding of the lengthy struggle they put up to protect that union.

2

Versatile Tractors

The Versatile tractor was the brainchild of Peter Pakosh, a Saskatchewan farm boy who grew up convinced that most farm equipment
was both too expensive and unnecessarily complicated. The child of
parents who emigrated from Poland to settle near Canora, Saskatchewan, in 1907, Pakosh was fascinated by farm equipment and was soon
maintaining and repairing the family implements. Raised as a Jehovah's
Witness, he travelled as an itinerant preacher after he graduated from
high school and before attending a technical engineering school in
Winnipeg in the early 1930s. Because there were no farm-implement
manufacturers in Winnipeg at the time, he moved to Toronto, where he
found work at Massey-Harris. Since Massey was not interested in
helping him develop his ideas for easy-to-maintain farm implements, he
designed and built a low-cost portable grain auger on his own, initially
working in the basement of his house. At one point, just to keep the new
business afloat, the cash-strapped company had to draw on the money
that his wife Adeline had been putting aside for a fur coat.

The product soon found a market in the Canadian prairies, and in
1947 Pakosh and his brother-in-law Roy Robinson, a machinist and
farmer, formed the Hydraulic Engineering Company. At the outset the
company manufactured augers, sprayers, and grain loaders, affixing all of
them with the Versatile brand name. In 1952, to be closer to the
Western Canadian and North-Central U.S. markets, the company moved
to Winnipeg.[1]

While Winnipeg had long been home to companies that made
wagons, sleighs, and small implements, it was not until the Second
World War that it developed a significant agricultural implement sector.
The prairie co-operative movement led the way in 1944, buying out a
small Winnipeg plant that had been producing horse-drawn farm implements and turning it into Canadian Co-operative Implements, a modern
manufacturing plant. Co-op Implements made a wide range of machinery, including combines, discers, and swathers. Later it sold imported
European tractors, including the Deutz and Volvo makes. In the early

1970s the firm employed over a thousand people, all members of the United Steelworkers, in its Transcona factory.[2]

When Pakosh and Robinson moved to Winnipeg they operated out of a plant on Main Street, and shortly afterwards opened a second plant on Plessis Road. Their company was incorporated as Versatile Manufacturing in 1963 and moved to a plant on Clarence Avenue in suburban Fort Garry the following year. With its forty-five acres of land to work with, the plant eventually expanded to cover fifteen acres. By the early 1960s Pakosh and Robinson had concluded that the company needed a full-scale tractor to complete its product line, and in 1966 Versatile became the first company to mass-produce four-wheel-drive tractors. These tractors, which became the backbone of the company, sold for the same price as their competitors' less powerful two-wheel-drive tractors. That same year Versatile also brought out a line of combines that quickly captured a significant share of the North American market.

These innovations underline two important aspects of the Versatile operation in the 1970s. First of all, the company made a heavy and continuous investment in research and development. Its experimental division brought together a highly skilled team of engineers and craft workers, capable of working together to create innovative and successful designs. Second, with a few exceptions such as engines and tires, almost all the parts that went into Versatile tractors were manufactured in the Fort Garry plant.

The decision to make tractors placed Versatile in the big leagues of the agricultural implement industry. In the 1970s dozens of companies were making swathers and augers, but only a handful of tractor manufacturers existed, and each of them had global reach. Between 1920 and 1950 the tractor revolutionized North American agriculture, and should have put to rest the stereotype of the farmer as the eternal conservative, averse to change. Its versatility and mobility promised to increase productivity, decrease labour costs, and even enhance the farmer's lifestyle by mechanizing a sector long characterized by back-breaking labour. The farmer embraced the tractor, with mixed results. Productivity did increase—to the point where a major problem in North American agriculture became overproduction. The tractor certainly was a labour-saving device, allowing farmers to cultivate ever larger farms, but then the farm's surplus labour had to leave for the city, accelerating the decline of rural communities. The farmer also became bound ever more tightly to the banker and international markets. No wonder that an Alberta farmer taking delivery of his new tractor in 1970 remarked that he now commanded "more field power, more comfort and convenience and more debt" than at any time in his farming career.[3] In the past if prices dropped, the farm family, and the horses and oxen that pulled the plough, could get by living on the food raised during the year. Once farmers started buying tractors and other major farm implements they lost this protection from the vagaries of the market. The cost of tractors increased so dramatically that many farmers could not afford the investment needed to stay in production. They could only retaliate by putting their tractor in the shop for the winter, giving it a thorough workover, and getting a few more years out of it. As a result, the tractor market itself has been subject to dramatic fluctuations.

The tractor itself goes back to 1892, when John Froelich of Iowa pieced together the first gasoline-powered machine for hauling and pulling farm equipment, using components purchased from local suppliers. It was another decade before Hart Parr, also of Iowa, began marketing the first commercially successful tractor. That same year, J.P. Morgan, the New York City financier who had overseen the creation of U.S. Steel and General Electric, merged the McCormick Harvesting Machine Company with four smaller machinery makers to create International Harvester (IH). By 1911 the Chicago-based International Harvester dominated the fledgling tractor industry, having captured a third of the U.S. market. That same year the J.I. Case Threshing Machine Company entered the field, only to discover that it was on the verge of its first collapse. Case survived, but in 1912 many small tractor companies that had not developed a distribution system or a market niche went out of business as supply outstripped demand.

Tractor manufacturing was still an easy business to get into: in 1916 more than 150 tractors were on the market, and in 1917 there were over 200 tractor manufacturers. Massey-Harris, Canada's largest farm-implement manufacturer, did not enter the field until 1918, when it reached an agreement with the Parrett Tractor Company of Chicago to manufacture Parrett tractors in Canada under the Massey-Harris name. The tractors failed to catch on with farmers, but in the late 1920s Massey entered into a much more successful agreement with J.I. Case.

The tractor world was transformed in 1917 when Henry Ford introduced his Fordson tractor. The first tractor produced on an assembly-line, the Fordson sold for $750, with a plough thrown in for good measure. In a stroke of marketing genius Ford announced that he had created the tractor as a part of his contribution to the war effort and would sell them only through state and provincial governments. In one year the Canadian government brought in over one thousand Fordsons, selling them through provincial governments. For Ford, a thousand tractors was a drop in the bucket: by 1920 over 100,000 North American farmers were using Fordsons.

The boom-and-bust nature of the tractor business was underlined by a 1921 sales collapse. U.S. tractor sales had hit an industry record of two hundred thousand in 1920, but as farm prices began to fall, farmers chose to sit tight and sales soon plummeted to twenty thousand. International Harvester fought back, launching what was to be a six-year price war with Ford. Throughout the 1920s both companies were prepared to lose over $300 on each tractor they sold. In 1928, IH overtook Ford in sales, and in the following year Ford took the Fordson off the market. In 1922 John Deere company executives had been thinking about getting the Moline, Illinois-based, company out of the tractor business entirely, but decided to stay the course. The next year the company introduced its Model D, a tractor that it was able to market successfully for three decades, ensuring Deere's long-term presence in the agricultural implement field. Far less successful were two companies based in Winnipeg, the Universal Farm Tractor Company and Sterling Company, which briefly manufactured tractors in the 1920s.

By the end of the Depression three companies—International Harvester, John Deere, and Allis-Chalmers—dominated the tractor sector. The other companies—Case, Oliver, Massey-Harris, Minneapolis-Moline, White Farm Equipment, and Cockshutt—simply played follow the leader. Farmers regularly complained about the lack of price competition, and inquiries conducted by the U.S. and Canadian governments backed them up. In 1938 the U.S. Federal Trade Commission (FTC) issued a highly critical assessment of the tractor-industry pricing structure, and International Harvester in particular. Some ten years later the tractor giants were still bullying their retailers into signing exclusive contracts that were illegal as well as harmful to local dealers. In 1948 the FTC initiated an anti-trust lawsuit against IH, but soon dropped the charges. As historian Robert C. Williams notes:

> A student of the industry summarized the process succinctly, "There are recognized 'market leaders' ... very large firms whose leadership in price setting is tacitly followed by others. Struggle between these giants takes the form of advertising, aggressive salesmanship, service and improvement of product, rather than price cutting." The existence of seven or more manufacturers has not resulted in price competition in North America.[4]

According to Williams, the other firms "simply priced their tractors and implements to compete with the two largest concerns, then adjusted production techniques until costs were considerably below the industry-wide price."[5]

Ford re-entered the tractor business in 1940 with a splash. A handshake agreement between Henry Ford and British inventor and industrialist Harry Ferguson led to the development of the Ford-Ferguson. A light, versatile machine, it captured 20 per cent of the tractor market in two years. Sales were so good that the Ford management was soon looking for a way to terminate its partnership with Ferguson. When the company found it could not force Ferguson out, it launched its own internal line of tractors in 1947, making use of Ferguson's still patented technical developments. Ferguson struck back with a quarter of a billion-dollar anti-trust lawsuit, winning $9.25 million in 1953. He took his money and his company and merged with Canada's Massey-Harris, creating the Massey-Ferguson Corporation.[6]

Meanwhile, the tractor was making a steady march across the prairies, as Grant MacEwan outlines in his history of farm implements in Western Canada:

> For all of Canada, tractor numbers rose from a mere 6 per 100 farms in 1921, to 14 per 100 farms in 1931, then 22 per 100 farms in 1941, and 64 per 100 farms in 1951. In the latter year, 70 per cent of all the tractors in Canada were in the three midwestern provinces, with the total number in the area almost equaling the total number of farms. For that three province area, there were 13 tractors per 100 farms in 1921, 29 per 100 farms in 1931, 38 per 100 farms in 1941, and 95 per 100 farms in 1951.[7]

North American sales peaked in 1965, and by the following year there were 160 tractors for every 100 farms on the Canadian prairies.[8] In 1977 there were 7 per cent fewer tractors in North America than there were in 1970,[9] and the implement industry was heading towards a major shake-down. By the early 1980s John Deere was selling nearly as many tractors as all of its competitors combined, and many of the companies were on the verge of bankruptcy. The manufacturers were the victims of a variety of pressures, including their own success. Tractors helped to make larger farms possible, but they also led to a decline in the number of farms, which cut the demand for tractors. International firms, particularly Kubota and Mitsubishi, were also making inroads into the North American market. In the 1980s hundreds of dealerships across North America failed.

A 60 per cent collapse in the tractor market between 1970 and 1983 pushed the entire industry to the edge. In the early 1980s low commodity prices and high interest rates drove down the demand for tractors. Deere laid off 40 per cent of its hourly employees; International Harvester and Massey-Ferguson faced bankruptcy; White Farm Equipment of Canada went bankrupt; and Allis-Chalmers and Case were losing money.[10] The Winnipeg-based Co-operative Implements was another victim of high interest rates and low prices. The *New York Times* speculated that names like Case, Massey-Ferguson, Allis-Chalmers, and even International Harvester might disappear—and most of them did. In 1985 International Harvester sold its farm equipment line to Case, and changed the name of its truck operation to Navistar Corporation. That same year Allis-Chalmers sold its farm equipment division to the German-based Klockner-Humboldt-Deutz (KHD). After a series of corporate transformations, KHD became AGCO in 1990. From its base outside Atlanta, Georgia, AGCO embarked on a series of takeovers, which saw it buy the White tractor line and Massey-Ferguson in 1994. The 1999 merger of New Holland and Case brought what was left of three of the major farm-implement companies—Case, Ford, and International Harvester—together under one corporate roof and left the industry with only two significant competitors, John Deere and AGCO.

Versatile was not immune to these shifts in fortune. In the early 1970s serious financial difficulties led the company to seek financial aid from Ed Schreyer's New Democratic Party government. Rather than loan Versatile money, the government hired future Liberal Party leader Izzy Asper to negotiate a share-purchase arrangement on its behalf. According to Sid Green, an NDP cabinet minister at the time, "The transaction was concluded but Versatile never drew on the funds. Instead it succeeded in arranging private financing on the strength of the government's commitment and overcame its financial difficulties."[11] By 1975 the company's founders, Peter Pakosh and Roy Robinson, were considering selling the plant to the Kansas-based Hesston Corporation, which was promising to invest $30 million in the plant and triple its manufacturing capacity and workforce. That offer was withdrawn before Canada's Foreign Investment Review Agency could vet it, but a year later the Vancouver-based Cornat Industries bought Versatile for $28 million. The announcement came just as Pakosh and Robinson were to receive the Canadian Industrial Development Award for 1976.[12] They had done well for two farm boys: at the time of the sale the company had 1,300 employees, sales of $100 million, and over 2,000 dealers around the world.[13] A third of its market was in the United States.[14]

Cornat Industries was a holding and management company with widely diversified investments that included shipyards, petroleum, real estate, warehousing, frozen food, finance, and trucking. Shortly after taking over Versatile, Cornat changed its corporate name to Versatile Corp. Its Winnipeg operation became Versatile Farm Equipment, and Cornat chief Peter Paul Saunders installed Paul Soubry as president of the plant. The Belgian-born Soubry had come to Manitoba as a teenager to work in his uncle's feed company in St. Boniface. He travelled to Ontario, where he worked for the Cockshutt Plow Company. He went to work for White Farm Equipment when it took over Cockshutt in 1962, eventually rising to the position of president. Soubry would remain at the helm of Versatile Farm Equipment until he retired at the end of 1995.[15] Scott McLaren, of the union, worked for Soubry for sixteen years, recalling that "the people on the floor had a lot of respect" for the company president. "In the times we were down and our place was up for sale, Paul Soubry seemed to be the guy who always found someone to buy us."

In the late 1970s, with support from the federal government, engineers at the plant developed a new, smaller bidirectional tractor with a cab that could swivel around completely, allowing farmers to work in tight areas. One of the most truly versatile tractors ever built, the bidirectional tractor offered the farmer tremendous accuracy and the option of using two implements, one at the front and one at the rear, at the same time. In keeping with Pakosh's original inspiration, it did not need to be broken down into several pieces to be serviced. Its design won the company tremendous loyalty through the farm community and a Design Canada award in 1984.

The success enjoyed by Versatile Farm Equipment provided a much-needed lifeline for Versatile Corporation. The parent company, it soon became apparent, was a house of cards that came crashing down: a victim of the recession of the early 1980s when the federal government drove interest rates into the double digits. Its petroleum and ship building investments went sour, costing the company millions of dollars. While the farm equipment provided over 40 per cent of the parent company's earnings, with the decline of demand sales fell from $340 million in 1981 to $208 million in 1983. In 1983 alone Versatile Corp. lost $23 million.[16]

In search of a needed infusion of cash, Versatile put its farm equipment division up for sale. In late 1985 Soubry announced an expected sale to John Deere, to be finalized early in the new year. The election of the Mulroney government in 1984 meant that there were no longer any barriers to foreign takeovers. The Foreign Investment Review Agency had been replaced by Investment Canada, and as the prime minister boasted, Canada was open for business.[17]

The news of the sale was too good to be true. John Deere was Versatile's chief competitor in the large tractor market. By taking over Versatile, it would control 80 per cent of the large tractor market. But even Ronald Reagan's America apparently had limits to the monopolization of the market. The U.S. Department of Justice put a stop to the sale and this would not be the last time that the U.S. Justice Department would play a decisive role in determining Versatile's future. Without a buyer, the Versatile plant all but closed down in 1986, and it appeared that that plant and its skilled workforce were lost to the province. The one glimmer of hope was the Ford Motor Company's 1985 decision to purchase Sperry New Holland, a Pennsylvania farm-implement company, creating Ford New Holland. Ford had always retained a tractor division, but much of the product that it sold in North America was manufactured in the United Kingdom. As the year progressed it became apparent that Ford New Holland was looking for a large tractor division, and its interest focused on Winnipeg. At the same time John Deere was assembling a new bid for the plant.

In February 1987 two federal cabinet ministers, Health Minister Jake Epp and Regional Economic Expansion Minister Michel Coté, walked onto the Versatile shop floor to announce that the plant had been saved. Coté told the workers that Ford New Holland was buying the plant, with a commitment to increase employment from 270 to 1,200 within five years. "With its new owners," Coté said, "Versatile will be given the world product mandate for research and development, and production and marketing of four-wheel-drive tractors. It will retain as well the mandate to produce the bidirectional tractors and swathers it has developed. Winnipeg will be the centre of research and development for Ford tractors." The dealer network open to Versatile would expand from 330 to nearly five thousand around the world. According to news reports Ford was paying $180 million for the plant, although little of the deal was in cash because Ford was taking over the liabilities of two Versatile-owned finance divisions and receiving a substantial loan from the Canadian government.

Even in its battered state, Versatile was hardly a piece of industrial debris. At the time of the Ford purchase it was Canada's only tractor manufacturer and the country's largest producer of farm implements, accounting for 25 per cent of Canada's farm-implement production. Over the previous eight years the company had enjoyed average domestic sales of $100 million and exports of $165 million.

In the end the key decision as to whether the sale would go to Ford or John Deere was made not by the ailing Versatile Corporation but by the federal cabinet. The night before the sale was announced, the cabinet had approved a $45.5-million loan, which was meant to assist Ford in purchasing the plant and modernizing its painting facility. The principal on this loan was to be paid back over ten years. The first payment would not come due until 1997, and Ford would not be required to make loan payments for periods in which the plant was not profitable. As an incentive to invest in the plant, Ford New Holland could avoid making any interest payments if it made minimum research and development and capital investments in the plant.

Kenneth Harrigan, president of the parent company, said Ford would have offered to purchase Versatile even without the loan. But, he said, the money "was available and we picked it up." The sale and the loan reflected that, beyond being open for business, the Canadian government no longer had a proactive national economic strategy. Not only was a valuable economic asset passing from Canadian to U.S. control, but the government was also financing the deal. While being owned by Ford would bring numerous benefits, key decisions about the plant's future would now be made in boardrooms in separate countries, and eventually on distant continents.

While the government and corporate officials were predicting a rosy future, Brian Chesnut, an analyst with the Richardson Greenshields investment firm, was not as optimistic. Prior to the merger Deere and Versatile had 80 per cent of the large tractor market, and this merger would only intensify what Chesnut saw as the industry's major problem: competition for market share. "If Deere had taken over Versatile, we would have had an amalgamation and a situation where the per unit cost of tractors would have dropped and the company would have been in a position to demand a price where it could make some money." The Ford takeover, Chesnut said, simply intensified competition between the two large companies.[18]

By 1990 the *Winnipeg Free Press* ran a story celebrating Versatile's return from the brink. With its 1,100 employees the company was making inroads into markets around the world, leading to a 35 per cent increase in the sale of four-wheel-drive tractors. New Holland had transferred the production of front-end loaders to Winnipeg from its plant in Romeo, Michigan. An $11-million remodelling had left the plant with a new paint line, a new paint oven, and a new conveyor system. Three assembly lines were running continuously, turning out

four-wheel-drive tractors, bidirectional tractors, and front-end loaders.[19]

A new decade, though brought a new recession. The workforce fell
to seven hundred, and in the spring of 1991 management announced
that it would be closing the plant three times between April and
October. To top matters off, Ford decided that it wanted to sell off most
of its investment in New Holland.[20]

In spring 1992 the Italian-based Fiat SpA corporation bought 80 per
cent of New Holland. Fiat was a company with a long and complicated
past. Started in 1899 by Giovanni Agnelli, a Piedmontese cavalry officer,
its early history was dotted with share swindles and allegations of cooked
books. The company's fortunes rose dramatically when Agnelli chose to
back a then-unknown political demagogue, Benito Mussolini.[21] After
Mussolini took power in Italy, one of his first acts was to halt a
government investigation into Fiat's war-profiteering during World
War One.[22] With government support and interests in finance, insurance, construction equipment, publishing, energy, trucks, aircraft engines, real estate, chemicals, telecommunications, defence electronics
and armaments, confectionery, and vermouth, Fiat came to dominate
Italian industry. It had nearly 200,000 employees worldwide and accounted for 5 per cent of the Italian economy. Fiat had also been making
agricultural machinery since 1919. Indeed, unlike companies in North
America, European automobile manufacturers have long made the manufacture of earth-moving equipment and farm implements a core part of
their operations.

By the early 1990s the company fell into trouble, after losing a third
of its share of the European car market. In 1993 the firm's bankers had to
arrange a $2.5-billion bailout of the company. The decline would have
been far worse had it not been for protection provided by the Italian
government in the form of limits on foreign imports and direct subsidies
to the company.[23] This political support had come at a price. In 1997
Fiat chairman Cesare Romiti, known as Il Duro (The Tough Guy), was
convicted of falsifying the company's accounts, committing tax fraud,
and illegally providing funding to political parties. The company's chief
financial officer was also convicted of working with Romiti to create a
slush fund that was funnelled to the company's political supporters.[24]

Not that Ford itself had a particularly unblemished history. Company founder Henry Ford was a virulent anti-Semite. His pamphlet *The
International Jew: The World's Foremost Problem,* won him the admiration
of Adolf Hitler and in 1938 the Grand Cross of the German Eagle. Ford
repaid the favour the following year with a gift to Hitler of 35,000

Reichsmarks on his birthday. After the Second World War broke out, Ford's plants in Germany and France turned out military vehicles for the Nazis with the active encouragement of the company's head office.[25] Ford also took a hard line with his North American workers. In 1932, when unemployed auto workers staged a march to protest their eviction from company-owned housing in Dearborn, Michigan, Ford enlisted the support of the local police. They fired on the crowd, leaving four men dead and fifty more seriously wounded.[26] As the nineteenth-century French novelist Honoré de Balzac noted, at the root of every great fortune lies a great crime.

The news stories announcing Fiat's takeover of Versatile were remarkably similar to those of five years earlier. Readers were told that the new owner intended to give Winnipeg the world production mandate for four-wheel-drive tractors, bidirectional tractors, and swathers. Within two years employment would be back up to 1,100, and the new owner—to be known simply as New Holland NV—might even transfer production of its two-wheel Genesis tractor from Antwerp to Winnipeg.[27] The federal loan was transferred to Fiat, which guaranteed its repayment. In 1993 the federal government loaned New Holland another $5.2 million to tool up for the promised Genesis production. Winnipeg was also to become the world hydraulic engineering platform for all of New Holland's tractors.

The change in ownership could not revive the farm economy. By the middle of 1992 350 workers were on permanent layoff and the future of a $10.6-million plant expansion was in doubt. In 1993 North American sales of four-wheel-drive tractors were down to 3,800 from 5,200 in 1991.[28]

By 1996 there was cause for cheer, as the ten-thousandth Genesis tractor produced by Versatile since the line had been transferred from Antwerp to Winnipeg rolled down the assembly line. Present at the celebrations were senior representatives of many of the Manitoba companies that supplied products for Versatile. These included Vansco Electronics, which claimed that it provided Versatile with the most advanced electronics system used by any tractor in the world, and Russel Metals, which had 25 per cent of its workforce involved in making steel frames for Versatile.[29]

In 1998 a New Holland publication boasted that the Winnipeg plant turned out thousands of tractors a year for customers in 180 countries. Over forty people were working in research and development, and the company was proud of its computer-aided design equipment, which meant that "all the work from initial concept through prototypes to production" was carried out "by their own people on powerful workstations." The same article touted the quiet, clean nature of production in the factory "due to the enlightened decision to use quiet torque converters to drive the hundreds of bolts instead of the more conventional and much louder impact wrenches." It remarked on the degree of labour force harmony: "There is precious little turnover and everybody seems to know each other's first names and are unfailingly polite in greeting one another." Each tractor was built to order: "The farmer specifies exactly what he or she wants with a dizzying array of choices: engine size, wheel size, number of wheels per hub and then there are dealer installed options."[30] But the article also indirectly hinted at a darker side to the Versatile story: for example, 70 per cent of the parts used at the plant came from outside manufacturers. The workers at the Versatile plant were no longer building tractors; increasingly they were assembling them. While the author mentioned the plant's employees had access to rows and rows of parking, he did not indicate that most of those spaces were empty. In September 1998 Versatile management announced what was intended to be an eight-week shutdown, laying off over five hundred workers. Plant vice-president Dave Morgan told the media that he had "every reason to be confident in the plant's future." As events unfolded over the next year it became apparent that such confidence was misplaced.

3

Who Builds Tractors?

Winnipeggers rarely connect south Winnipeg with factory work or assembly lines. The city's fabled North End, which lies on the wrong side of the giant Canadian Pacific freight yards, and the portion of the downtown just south of those yards comprise the city's traditional industrial heartland. Over time many of the industries there moved to industrial parks, or simply disappeared. The community south of the Assiniboine River is, in the city's political geography, the home of the elite, not its factories. Few Winnipeggers, even those who live and work in south Winnipeg, would have occasion to clap eyes on the Versatile tractor plant, located on its forty-five acres in an industrial park in suburban Fort Garry. To most observers it might simply be a giant warehouse or parts depot.

Most Winnipeggers in the 1990s would probably have heard of Versatile, but they may not have known that the company was the last remaining tractor plant in Canada, let alone one of only five such plants in all of North America. During that decade economic attention was turned elsewhere, to the computer and the Internet, the arrival of the so-called new knowledge-based economy. The self-employed innovator was the model for the future; the blue-collar worker who wanted a job for life was a doomed and pitiable dinosaur.

Today the new economy has come and largely gone, leaving in its wake a tangle of lawsuits, frauds, and pilferings—all a needed reminder that no matter which economy we move to next, manufacturing is going to matter. Operations such as Versatile will continue to be key to a community's economic success. From the outset Peter Pakosh, a true innovator, was able to attract a strong core of engineers interested in the opportunity to design and develop new tractors. Design engineers were always essential to the company's success. Until the time it was sold, Versatile engineers were using the latest in computer-design equipment to continue to modify and develop the company's product line.

Casual television viewers in the 1990s might have wondered if anyone other than a computer programmer had a hope of ever getting a job in the economy of the future. They might well have come to the conclusion that factory work was inherently bad, or the reserve of the thick-witted and the burly. Unions, except for when they are on strike, are also rarely in the public eye. Nowadays you often hear people say that while unions might have been needed in the past, the problems they were confronting have all been solved. To the degree that this opinion has any validity, it is a testament to the labour movement's accomplishments, not to its current irrelevancy. It also explains why workers are often so attached to their unions.

In the course of researching this book I interviewed nearly two dozen former Versatile workers, all of them men, usually in their homes. Most of them lived in Winnipeg's working-class suburbs—some in Transcona, some in St. Vital, some in the North End. Their homes were often relatively new and well maintained, a silent tribute to both the value of manufacturing jobs and the ability to win decent wages through union contracts. There was nothing ostentatious about the homes or these men's lifestyles; over the decades spent at Versatile they had managed to accumulate some of the badges of membership in the Canadian middle class. They had their cars, appliances, living-room and dining-rooms suites, televisions and stereos. To interview them I sat at the inevitable kitchen table, with the inevitable filter coffee machine close at hand, and I saw the usual signs of family—children coming in and out, framed photographs of graduations and marriages. The men often spoke of the difficulties that going on strike had created for them, especially when they were trying to help their children through university. They were model citizens, with gardens they cultivated, lawns they watered and trimmed, neighbours they chatted with. Unless you knew otherwise, you wouldn't be able to tell if they were cooks or accountants on their days off. They didn't seem at all like the stereotypical blue-collar worker. What they had most in common was that together they made tractors and created a union.

Even the most skilled engineers don't build tractors on their own. Versatile needed dozens of skilled machinists, people who could take a piece of paper and turn it into a working prototype. These workers came from all over the world. One of them, Ed Balik, was trained as a mechanical engineering technologist in his native Poland. By 1970 he was working in the engine room of a boat that sailed far and wide to supply the Polish fishing fleet. When the fleet docked in Halifax, Balik jumped ship and claimed refugee status. Relatives helped him move to Winnipeg, where he found a job as a tool-and-dye maker in Versatile's experimental division. To this day he retains strong and positive memories of his early years at Versatile. "I was very pleased from day number one," he told me. "I was working with some hope for the future, with some hope that I would be able to improve my life here. And over there in Poland was no hope." At Versatile his skills won him respect: on many occasions the engineers would come to the machinists and ask them if it would be possible to build a component in a certain fashion. "We would tell them we would give it a try. Today, I still feel proud when I see a Versatile tractor in the field and can say to myself, 'I helped create the prototype for that tractor.'"

Louis Mora came to Canada five years after Ed Balik, also as a political refugee. A surveyor by training, he had held a political appointment as a housing official in Salvador Allende's socialist government in Chile. Allende came to power in 1970 as the head of the Popular Unity coalition. Mora was a member of the Movement for United Popular Action (MAPU), a political party made up largely of young people who had left the more conservative Christian Democratic Party; it was also a part of the Popular Unity coalition. Mora joked as he tried to explain the complexities of Chilean politics: "You put two Chileans together, they form a party." The fate of the Allende government is no laughing matter; it was overthrown by a violent military coup in September 1973. Allende was killed while defending the presidential palace, and thousands of his supporters were arrested. Many of them were never heard from again.

During the early days of the coup, Mora decided not to go into hiding. He was naïve, he said, telling himself then, "I did not do anything wrong. Why do I have to hide? Everything I did was right. I was not the sort of person who only favoured people from the party." The military dictatorship made no such distinctions: Mora was arrested and spent nearly two years in a concentration camp before friends of his in Toronto, working with the Canadian government, won his release. He got help and protection from the Canadian embassy and the Catholic Church. "I was given two hours to say good-bye to my mother and my auntie, and an embassy official took me to the airport and he was there until my plane left." After arriving in Canada he moved to Winnipeg.

Mora ended up at Versatile by chance. A friend phoned him up to say he had a job interview at Versatile the next day but couldn't go because he had just been hired to work at the Griffin Steel foundry in Transcona. He suggested that Mora go for the interview in his stead. Mora went, got the job, and started at the company's plant on Plessis Road, working as a helper in the paint shop. "It was very difficult," he said. At first he couldn't speak the language, and he had been a surveyor, not a labourer. As he picked up the language and skills needed for work in the paint shop, Mora also began to understand how the plant operated. "There was plenty of favouritism. You might know how to do a job and apply for the promotion, but they would give it to someone else they liked. And then you had to train that person to do the job that they would not hire you to do." Mora worked in the paint shop for twenty-five years.

Many of the Versatile workers came from countries that had once been part of the British Empire. Joseph Smith, for example, was from Trinidad, where he had served a five-year apprenticeship and worked as lathe operator for the Texaco Corporation. In search of a better life for his children, he moved his family to Canada in 1967 and soon found work in the Versatile toolroom. It was, he said, a place where you could approach any member of management with your concerns. When asked point blank if it was a good place to work, he levelled his gaze, making it clear that he had skills and ability. If it had not been a good place, he would have taken his skills and gone elsewhere.

Winston Johnson came to Canada in the early 1980s from Guyana, where he had undergone a five-year apprenticeship as a machinist. A number of Johnson's friends in the South American country had already come to Canada, and he decided to join them. He soon started work at Versatile as a machinist. In those early years the company was a good place to work, but he soon recognized that promotions were generally granted to those who were on good terms with the foremen.

Ray Wilkie Sr. came to Canada from Jamaica in 1973, and two years later he went to work as a maintenance electrician at Versatile. Before starting with Versatile he worked on the construction of the town complex in Churchill, Manitoba. Like many Versatile workers, over the years he moved through various departments in the plant, including an assembly-line job and working in stores as a forklift operator. He too recalled the favouritism prevalent in many departments in the early days. "If you were buddy-buddy with the foreman you would get preference, you would get more money than the other guy, even if you were doing the same job. And if you were on layoff and the foreman did not like you, other people would get recalled before you." Buddy-buddy is a term that many Versatile workers used to describe the company's promotion policies in the early years—and it was always used with disdain.

Surinder Brar was born in India, where his father was an army officer and other family members were small farmers. After coming to Canada in the early 1970s Brar, who became known as Sandy, worked in a

British Columbia sawmill along with a number of relatives and friends. While there, they helped to organize the workers into a local of the International Woodworkers of America. In 1974 Brar and his friends, dismayed by the level of racial hostility they experienced on the West Coast, headed east, with the intent of moving to Toronto. They stopped in Winnipeg to visit with friends, and decided, despite the cold, to look for work. Brar and his cousin George both found jobs at Versatile, where Brar started as an assembler on the transmission assembly line.

Many other Versatile employees came from rural Manitoba. Indeed, Pakosh and Robinson were willing to allow farmers to work in the plant for part of the year and take time off in the other part to attend to crops. The practice generated tremendous loyalty. Other country boys moved to the city and took full-time work at Versatile. Bill Sokoliuk, from the town of Sundown, got his job as a bellhop at the St. Regis Hotel on Smith Street back in the days when the St. Regis was the home away from home for rural members of the Manitoba legislature. From the St. Regis he went to work on the CNR dining cars, making $2.66 an hour. After he got married he decided to give up travelling and took a job in the Versatile machine shop. Like many Versatile workers, he not only knew the year he started with the company, but also knew the date: April 13, 1966. He was twenty-one years old, and his job was running the automatic lathe and drills. "When I started we did all the machining for our tractors. They even made their own gears for transmissions." At the start of his career with Versatile he made $1.66 an hour and put in a forty-eight-hour week. "We didn't know any better, and we thought it was great."

While he thought Robinson and Pakosh were fair men, he believed they favoured other Jehovah's Witnesses when it came to hiring and promotion. "It was made clear to you that you would do better if you were a Jehovah's Witness." While some foremen actually held prayer meetings in the plant, others were more interested in spirits than in their co-workers' spiritual salvation. "One supervisor wanted you to give him a bottle of whiskey before he would give you a good shift." Sokoliuk would have liked to work better shifts, but there was no way he was going to bribe his supervisor. "For a bottle of whiskey I am not going to work days." Like other Versatile employees he was proud of the company product. "They loved it. They loved it. I'm telling you, the people working there loved it. It was what was behind it—it was really a good machine."

Len Rausch, who grew up on a farm near Dauphin, Manitoba, went to work for the CNR in 1969 as a high-steel rigger and welder. During his years on the railroad he spent much of his time on the road, maintaining railway bridges or working the power shops at the Symington Yards in Transcona. A couple of years after getting married in 1976 he decided that he needed to stay closer to home. After working for a while in a metal shop on Wall Street, in 1979 he parlayed a childhood friendship with the personnel manager at Versatile into a welding job. Rausch was also proud of the work done at Versatile: "We were always ahead of everybody else because we started ahead of everybody else. We did all our own stuff. The only thing we never did was our motors and our alternators." In Rausch's estimation, "The reason why farmers like Versatile products is because you could rip the whole thing apart right there in the field because of its modular design. Whereas a John Deere could be in a shop for weeks."

In the early 1980s another generation of workers appeared on the scene. They were more likely to be city kids, figuring to stay for a few years and then move on. Scott McLaren was twenty years old when he started working in the Versatile stores department in January 1980, and at the time he only expected to work there for a few years. He came from a farm family, although his father had left the farm to work for the Canadian Wheat Board. He got his job because a friend of his mother's knew the plant manager, Reg Honeyborne. He recalled the early 1980s as an incredibly busy time at Versatile. They couldn't make tractors fast enough—and they were turning out about eighteen large four-wheel-drive tractors a day. "Every one that we made we knew who the farmer was, where it was going. There was none of this make some stock and see if they sell." During those years employees were never idle. "If you stood still for more than a minute somebody handed you a broom or a shovel." The workforce, he said, was knowledgeable and well trained. "You really have to give the family credit for that. They made sure people were trained to do their jobs." Tom McCallum, who worked with McLaren as a forklift operator in those days, said: "I remember when I first started in the spot-welding there were two forklift operators and there were thirty-two workers you had to keep supplied. It was like a rat race. The working conditions were just whip and chain and go, go, go. When you are young your stamina allows you to handle it."

Paul Lussier started on the Versatile assembly line in 1980, when he was nineteen years old. An older brother who had worked there before him gave the company a mixed assessment, telling him the pay was good, but it was not that good a place to work. The younger brother concurred with that assessment. "They didn't have proper ventilation, machine safeguarding [was] non-existent, and if they told you to do something you were just expected to do it and not question the company on it." Once again, Lussier reported that promotions "were done strictly by who you knew and if they liked you. The company more or less did what it wanted to do, with total disregard for the employees."

Dwight Pitcher had moved to Winnipeg on March 19, 1979, and started work at Versatile a week later. At the time he knew little about tractors or mechanics. But a foreman recognized his aptitude and within two years Pitcher was working as a tractor mechanic, a job he loved, with products he admired. Later on Pitcher spent five years working on special projects at Versatile and was deeply involved in the development of a new version of the Genesis tractor. In his basement Pitcher has hundreds of photographs of the tractors that he helped to build from scratch, going through a dozen versions in the planning process. "The first one was made of cardboard, the second one was made of cardboard and plaster, the third one had a real axle and real cab." The fourth version would actually run, and the process would go on and on from there. The tractor cost $40 million to develop "and took two years to get on line."

The Versatile workers were represented by an employees association, the Hydraulic Engineering Workers Association (HEWA). The name dated back to the days when the company was known as Hydraulic Engineering—there were no engineers in the association itself. HEWA, an independent organization, did not organize workers at any other plant and was not affiliated with any other labour union or federation. Its dues were low and it had no strike fund. Many of its leaders had been with the company since it moved to Winnipeg in the 1950s, and they believed that the Association and Versatile had reached an accommodation that worked for both parties. After the 1976 sale to Cornat— although Robinson remained involved with plant management—it was clear that the old days of paternalism had come to an end. By the early 1980s layoffs were becoming common, wages were under attack, and the future of the company seemed uncertain. Frustration with HEWA began to grow.

In his time with the railway Len Rausch had been an active member of the Brotherhood of Maintenance of Way Employees. He knew first-hand that wages and benefits were better on the railway than at Versatile, and he did not think much of the Versatile working conditions. "It could be very hot and smoky. There were 239 welders working at one time and you couldn't recognize a forklift driver from twenty feet—

that's how bad the smoke was." Nor did he think that HEWA could do much to change things. "The Association really was not able to force the company to do anything that it did not want to do." He said that the management rights clause, which outlined the areas over which management had exclusive authority, "was a page and a half long."

Lussier likewise had little respect for the Association. While HEWA had bargained some limited seniority rights for the workers, those rights lapsed after a worker had been laid off for six months. Lussier said that once he was not recalled until the day after his seniority rights lapsed. He was bitter that the Association could not provide any better protection. Joseph Smith, who had experience as a shop steward with the oil-field workers union in Trinidad, realized after he had been with Versatile for a while that HEWA "wasn't really a union." It had no bite, he said. "Whatever the management recommended, they had to go along with that." Ray Wilkie agreed: "Well, there was a lot of favouritism and you had no security, you had no pension, you had no benefits, you had no strength." In bargaining with the Association the company would say "This is the last offer, take it or leave it." HEWA "had no strike fund," Wilkie said. "They had nothing so you know we just had to take it." Still, while Winston Johnson did not think much of the HEWA, he believed its leaders "were working guys who wanted to do the right thing but didn't have the background, didn't have the training. So there was no proper representation for the membership there."

Stan Letwyn started with Versatile in 1980 as a drill-press operator in the machine shop. Believing that hard workers would be protected from layoffs, he did not see much value in seniority systems that say that the last hired is the first to be laid off. His views changed when he saw how the company manipulated the minimal seniority guarantees negotiated by HEWA. Shortly after he and a number of other younger workers were transferred to different departments, the company laid off a number of workers in Letwyn's old department. "They were letting guys go that they didn't like even though they had ten to fifteen years' seniority, and keeping me there with three or four years' seniority." Letwyn concluded, "No matter what your loyalty was to the plant, if you weren't doing what they wanted or you argued with them or whatever, or for whatever reason they didn't like you, you were gone and they put in a younger guy right off the street. That's when I changed over to believe in the seniority system."

Tom McCallum admitted that when he started at Versatile he was "young and snotty." When he got into trouble with management, he concluded that the Association would not be able to do much for him. "I took them one problem and they just laughed. You never really got anything for your money. If you complained it was never heard—it was pretty much a company organization. I could never see a pension coming out of HEWA. They were not striving for benefits."

Jaime De La Rosa, a welder who later served on the CAW Local executive, decided to support campaigns to bring in an outside union because he believed that HEWA was not doing a good job for the members. "You ask them to do something for you and then you have to wait days before they act, or sometimes they just forget about it." Sometimes, De La Rosa said, HEWA would say, "Oh we can't do nothing about that." To get overtime, he said, a worker had to be "buddy-buddy with the foreman." If you just wanted to do your job, you were in trouble.

Scott McLaren, who served as a HEWA shop steward and went on to play a leading role in the CAW, was not as critical of the Association as others were. He thought that the Association did the best it could with its limited resources: "Remember, we were only paying three dollars a month in dues. There was not much the Association could do with that." He saw a strong division between those who remained loyal to the Association and the younger workers who wanted to bring in an outside union. According to McLaren, "A lot of these guys had worked for the company from 1950 when it was a family-owned place and treated people fairly well although you worked very hard at Versatile. You had a lot of people who were loyal to the family, and even though the family had been gone a long time they were still loyal to the business." After McLaren had been on the job for six months, management laid off some workers who had been there for thirty years but kept him on because he had a licence to operate a forklift. McLaren knew that many of the workers who had been laid off could easily have been trained to run a forklift. "I just happened to get lucky and get hired into a department that hardly ever got laid off and managed to stick for many years until we got pure seniority at Versatile." To win promotion workers had to pass certain tests, but McLaren began to suspect that the company was providing answers to the tests to workers it wanted to promote. In McLaren's mind these instances of unfairness and favouritism had an impact on every worker in the plant. "Guys who had been there for thirty years were going out the door. The need for seniority was what brought the union in."

Rausch and McCallum also had stories to tell of older workers being laid off while newly hired employees were kept on. Rausch was laid off once early on in his time at Versatile, but there were times when men who had been there for far longer were laid off while he kept on working. It didn't seem at all fair, McCallum recalled. "I got to admit I kept my job pretty steady. I was a young hard worker and they kept you. And if you were laid off they brought you back first."

Another problem was that by the 1980s Versatile workers were beginning to retire—and they would immediately fall upon hard times. The Versatile pension was so low that people with thirty years' experience had pensions as low as $30 a month.

An increasing number of Versatile workers were convinced that they needed a union, one with experience in negotiating and enforcing industrial contracts and with the financial resources to back them up in the event of a strike. The question was, which union was right for farm-implement workers?

In the late nineteenth century farm-implement companies were among the largest employers in North America. In 1884 Cyrus McCormick employed 1,400 workers in Chicago. In the 1880s the Massey plant in Toronto, with over 700 workers, was the city's largest employer. These workers were among the first to join unions. In 1886 workers at Toronto's Massey plant, members of the Knights of Labor, approached their managers with two demands: they wanted a copy of the wage rate, and they wanted the right to be paid every two weeks rather than on a monthly basis. The company not only denied their request, but also fired six of the workers who had joined the Knights of Labor, claiming that as a matter of policy the company would not employ anyone who belonged to a union. Daniel O'Donoghue, one of the Knights' leading figures in Toronto, was not certain whether the union could win a strike, but as he wrote to the organization's international leader Terence Powderly, the union had little choice in the matter.

> I saw that it was better in this case to risk a contest and all it implied than to desert the men who faced Massey on the strength of their faith in their brothers and the Order in general. Not to have taken the action would have ruined our character. Better far honorable defeat than that it should be said that we had not the pluck to defend our existence and the rights even of the few.[1]

To the surprise of both Massey and O'Donoghue, four hundred members of the Knights of Labour walked off the job. Within a week the strike was over and the men were back on the job—and Massey even promoted a leading figure in the union to the position of foreman.[2]

Unfortunately, the Knights were unable to resist the double whammy of an employer counterattack and an economic recession. By the 1890s the organization was in rapid decline, and by the early twentieth century it had all but disappeared—as had unionism in the farm-implement industry.

In the mid-1880s, McCormick invested half a million dollars in new equipment that would allow it to carry on production without skilled moulders. The company then provoked a bitter strike and drove the union out. In 1890 Massey told its moulders not to bother returning to work unless they agreed to a pay cut. The union lost a lengthy strike, during which many of its members were arrested for intimidating strikebreakers.[3] The International Association of Machinists, with the support of the Chicago Federation of Labor, was able to establish itself at International Harvester in the early years of the twentieth century, but in 1905 after closing down for two weeks, IH reopened on a completely non-union basis.[4] In 1919 five thousand IH workers struck, unsuccessfully, to re-establish the union, and International Harvester and the rest of the industry would remain union-free until the 1930s and 1940s.[5]

In the twentieth century the farm-implement companies began to experiment with carrots as well as sticks to keep unions out. International Harvester developed an elaborate corporate welfare system, although it made sure that benefits were not available to workers who went on strike or joined a union. Its system often included a works council, an elaborate grievance system that operated within rules laid down by the company. Not surprisingly these councils were often referred to as company unions. Historian Irving Bernstein describes them as "the most important device employers used to prevent or undermine labour organizations."[6] International Harvester's Cyrus McCormick III declared that councils "gave workers an opportunity of deliberating upon and practically deciding their own destiny." The corporation maintained veto power over council decisions, despite McCormick's claim that the worker and the employers' interests were "one and the same."[7] When the workers on the Council wanted a pay increase in the 1920s, the company turned them down flat.[8]

In Canada Massey-Harris also had its own work council. When worker members on the council proposed in 1923 that a 20 per cent pay cut be rescinded, the company president appeared at the next council meeting to explain that it would not be possible to increase wages, although there might be adjustments in some piecework and day rates. It was, as historian Bruce Scott notes, a position that "committed the company to practically nothing, and seemed to absolve the management delegates in the council from any responsibility for the refusal of the original request."[9] At Massey-Harris the company found that it was increasingly difficult to get workers to participate in the council, which, according to Scott, was not surprising given that "the council did not alleviate in any way the basic insecurity of employment caused by the annual shutdowns and the variability of agricultural production in Canada and elsewhere."[10]

The turning point for industrial workers came in the mid-1930s. Throughout the early years of the decade young members of the Communist Party had been trying with little success to organize all workers in industrial plants, regardless of skill, in Canada and the United States. While most of the leaders of the craft unions continued to believe that unskilled and semi-skilled workers were unorganizable, a few far-sighted union leaders had concluded that the future of the union movement rested in organizing all skilled and unskilled workers. They did not envision creating one big union, but they did believe that there should be, for example, one union for meat packers, one for auto workers, one for steelworkers, and one for electrical workers. When the American Federation of Labor (AFL) refused to embrace this one-industry, one-union model, mineworkers president John L. Lewis led a walk out of the AFL convention to establish the Committee for Industrial Organization (CIO), which later became the Congress of Industrial Organizations. The CIO hired many of the young communist activists who had been trying to build an industrial union movement and provided them with the resources and support they needed. The fledgling CIO developed a powerful new weapon, the sit-down strike. In January 1936 striking workers at the Firestone plant in Akron, Ohio, occupied their plant. The strike established the union and inspired auto workers to stage a similar strike at the General Motors plant in Flint, Michigan. The month-long plant occupation in Flint ended in a victory and established the CIO-affiliated United Automobile Workers (UAW).

Shortly after the CIO's formation, Canadian communist trade-union activist J.B. Salsberg travelled to the United States to see if the Congress could send some organizers to Canada. The Congress, without enough organizers even to meet the needs of U.S. workers, turned down the request. In the end the CIO was created in Canada by industrial workers determined to share in the benefits that they saw their brothers and sisters winning south of the border.

The breakthrough came in February 1937, when General Motors introduced an assembly-line speed-up at its Oshawa plant. In response to frantic phone calls, the UAW headquarters in Detroit dispatched Hugh Thompson, who organized a Canadian local of the UAW. A month later Local 223 in Oshawa had over four thousand members led by Charlie Millard, the president of the local committee of the Co-operative Commonwealth Federation, the forerunner of the New Democratic Party. When the company announced that it would not negotiate with the union as long as it was affiliated to the CIO, a strike became inevitable.

On April 8, 1937, GM's four thousand Oshawa employees walked off the job. The strike and union came under a barrage of criticism from Ontario Premier Mitchell Hepburn, who labelled it "the first attempt on the part of Lewis and his CIO henchmen to assume the position of dominating and dictating to Canadian industry."[11] As matters dragged on, the union and the strike were on the verge of collapse, but General Motors was eager to get back to producing cars. A compromise was reached: GM would sign an agreement with Millard, and he, in turn, would sign a statement indicating that he did not represent the CIO. This victory established the United Auto Workers in Canada. In the coming years the union would go on to organize all of the Big Three auto makers, becoming one of the largest unions in Central Canada and a powerful player in the Canadian labour movement.

At the same time that Canadian auto workers were joining the UAW, Grant Oakes and Joe Weber, two young communist activists, were creating the Farm Equipment Organizing Committee (FECO) in the United States. Oakes had worked for International Harvester's giant Tractor Works and served for a while on the company-initiated work council before quitting in disgust. Before the year was out Oakes and Weber had won a major organizing victory at International Harvester. The following year the FECO was transformed into the United Farm Equipment and Metal Workers Union, usually known as the FE. It was not until 1941 that the FE was able to bring the majority of workers at International Harvester and Allis-Chalmers under contract.[12] By the mid-1940s the union had eighty thousand members. According to historian Toni Gilpin:

> Within the FE, no action was deemed unacceptable if it contrib-
> uted to the favorable resolution of a worker's grievance. While
> many unions endorsed contract language prohibiting strikes
> during the life of their agreement, the FE generally refused to
> instruct union members who walked off the job to return to work.
> In fact, Harvester often charged that the FE encouraged or

sponsored such "wildcat" strikes. FE members, indeed, readily walked off the job to settle disagreements. Harvester plants represented by the FE experienced 849 work stoppages between 1945 and 1951.[13]

The union's reputation for feisty radicalism was well deserved, but it became caught up in and eventually destroyed by the era's Cold War politics. CIO president John L. Lewis was once asked by U.S. Secretary of Labor Frances Perkins if he was disturbed by the number of Communist Party members in leadership positions in CIO unions. Lewis, a staunch anti-communist, responded with an analogy from the world of hunting: who got the bird, the hunter or the dog? Once the communists had built the CIO, he said, they would be discarded. Indeed, in the late 1940s the U.S. and Canadian labour movements began to purge Communist Party members from union office, while unions with communist leadership were expelled from the CIO and its Canadian counterpart, the Canadian Congress of Labour. The FE was expelled in 1949, and the United Auto Workers mounted an intense campaign intended to win FE members away from their union. In 1952 the FE lost a bitter strike at International Harvester, and in 1955 a badly battered FE admitted defeat and merged with the UAW.[14] From that point on the UAW represented most of the unionized farm-implement workers in the United States and Canada. It would, however, be thirty years before the union successfully organized the Versatile tractor workers.

When they began talking up the idea of joining a union in the early 1980s, the Versatile workers did not turn immediately to the UAW. Len Rausch approached his old union, the Maintenance of Way Employees, but they showed no interest in taking on the challenge. In the end, with Peter Magda playing a key role, the workers asked the United Steelworkers of America to launch an organizing drive. Paul Lussier recalled it as a hard-fought campaign in which the company told the workers that they would lose their jobs if the Steelworkers were certified. At one point several people were fired for handing out union cards on company time. The union fought the dismissals at the labour board, but was not able to get all the workers reinstated. The company then laid aside its sticks and brought in a dollar an hour raise, effectively taking the wind out of the Steelworker campaign.

Louis Mora remembered with a rueful laugh how one of his co-workers told him that the wage increase was enough to convince him not to support the union. A few months later that worker's wife had serious dental problems. "I told him what he really needed now was a union dental plan, not a dollar an hour raise."

The defeat of the Steelworker campaign coincided with an expansion of the UAW into Western Canada. Prior to the 1980s the Auto Workers were all but non-existent in Manitoba, representing workers in a number of small manufacturing plants serviced out of an office in Thunder Bay. In 1980 the union succeeded in winning the right to represent workers at the Boeing plant in Winnipeg. In the following year Hemi Mitic moved to Winnipeg to set up the union's Winnipeg office and serve as the UAW's Western Canadian organizer. Mitic had heard about Versatile before he came to Winnipeg, and it seemed logical to give it a try. When people kept telling him, "You'll never organize that plant," it only served to heighten his determination.

Before the union rented its own office, Mitic worked out of a small office provided to him by Gary Doer, the president of the Manitoba Government Employees' Association (MGEA) at the time. Looking back on the organizing drive, Mitic said that Doer's support was instrumental in the campaign's success. Doer not only gave him an office, he gave him the keys to the building and said, "whatever equipment, whatever paper you need, you just go ahead and use it." Whenever something of moment happened at the labour board or in the plant, Mitic said, "We would go down to the MGEA, put together a leaflet, and run off thirteen hundred copies in minutes." Then they'd rush down to the plant to hand out the leaflets.

Mitic started by approaching HEWA president Ron Lee in hopes of bringing the Association into the UAW. When the Association leaders made it clear that they had no interest in the UAW, Mitic began signing up Versatile members, starting with forklift driver Stan Kusiak. The union kept a low profile, never spreading around word about who had signed cards. "People were really afraid of losing their jobs. That's always the case, but for whatever reason this was one of the most secretive campaigns in the early stages that I've ever been around." Winston Johnson later commented that he had been impressed by the union's discretion. Mitic soon came to realize that this was an incredibly diverse workforce. Not only did it have Filipino, Portuguese, Caribbean, Chilean, East Indian, and Francophone contingents, but each ethnic group also contained cross-currents: Filipino workers who supported Marcos, Filipino communists who opposed Marcos, and other Filipinos who opposed both Marcos and the communists.

The plant was so large that Mitic got permission to hire Barrie Farrow on as a temporary organizer. Farrow, who worked at a Ford parts distribution centre on Ellice Avenue in Winnipeg and was president of the amalgamated UAW local in the city, discovered that he had a passion and a gift for organizing. He particularly loved making house calls, usually putting in a dozen or more a day. "Going up to the house I didn't know what to expect or what the issues were going to be," he said. "With some people it was seniority. Some people just hated their foreman. For some people it was more money." With the issues varying from person to person, he found it was not at all a matter of people saying, "everybody wants a union because of greed." Once in the door, Farrow would quickly try to establish a rapport. "If the guy had a guitar I'd talk about the guitar. If he had a stereo I'd talk about the stereo for two or three minutes." His goal was to get the card signed on the first visit. He brought it out early in the visit, let the worker read it, touch it, ask questions about it. "Signing the card is just the first step in bringing a person into the union, so I had to work to get that initial commitment."

As a means of ensuring that workers were actually making a commitment to the union, the Manitoba labour code required that the union collect a dollar from each member who signed a card—and the union was not allowed to loan the dollar to the worker. One night a worker told Farrow he would sign the card, but he did not have the dollar.

> I looked around and saw all these pop bottles. I said, "Are those yours?" He says, "Yeah." I said, "Count me out some pop bottles, I'll take them and I'll turn them in and give you what they're equivalent to." I went and got money for those pop bottles, said, "That's your money, I didn't lend it to you, sign the card."

From Farrow's perspective, HEWA was similar to most in-house organizations in that its key people started out believing they could help to make a difference but ended up being tied to the company. As Farrow recalled, the Association tried to portray itself as the victim of a takeover by the big strong outside union. Unfortunately for the Association, many people saw the UAW's strength and size, particularly when compared to HEWA, as an advantage. Aside from winning people away from the Association, the other big challenge of the Versatile drive was the fluctuating level of employment. Farrow kept four separate lists of Versatile employees—active employees, workers on layoff, workers on compensation, and a miscellaneous group—and watched carefully as workers moved from group to group. "We had to know how many of our cards were valid at any time, and who might be eligible to vote."

Lussier was impressed with the UAW organizers. "Mitic and Farrow and the people around them were a close-knit group of people who believed deeply in what they were doing."

At the time Len Rausch was a lead hand. "I had the respect of the ethnic groups in there, treated them half-decently, and most management didn't treat them at all well. I figured everybody had a brain and probably they could be a lead hand too." The Filipino workers told the UAW organizers that they would not join unless Rausch signed up. When UAW organizer Al Seymour showed up on his doorstep a few days later, Rausch told him, "I'll help you out, but if we fail the first time and you guys take off, you'll never get back in again as long as I'm there." Seymour told him, "If we fail the first time we'll back off for six months and we'll hit it again." That was good enough for Rausch, who was soon signing up most of the welding workers right in the plant. At one point in the drive Rausch was in the UAW office for a meeting with the union's fabled Canadian director Bob White, who asked him how many signed cards he had. Rausch gave a vague and tentative answer, leading White to cut in: "Look, don't give me any shit. I asked you how many cards you got signed? How many you got right now?" To which Rausch deadpanned, "Why didn't you say so?"

In Farrow's mind, Magda and Rausch were key people in the organizing campaign. He recalled Magda as a charger. "He would go up and down the line talking up the union and every few nights he would come in with a big stack of signed union cards." According to Farrow, Magda could keep his calm only for so long when he was approaching workers. Soon enough he would say, "I've asked you three times this week, when are you going to join the union?" Rausch "would just grind people down. He would go at you slowly. He directed us to a lot of the older guys. He had a lot of credibility in the plant."

Government-appointed labour boards were established in Canada in the 1940s, when the federal government recognized, in the face of a wave of illegal strikes, that the labour movement was going to be a permanent part of the Canadian industrial landscape. New labour relations rules required employers to bargain with unions that had been certified by a labour board (usually made up of a government appointee, a labour appointee, and an employer appointee). Labour boards could only certify those unions that had the support of the majority of workers in a defined bargaining unit. This sometimes lengthy and legalistic approach replaced the old system in which unions usually had to go on strike to force an employer to bargain with them and employers could legally fire people simply for being union members. Once a union is certified, only a limited number of windows of opportunity exist during which another union can challenge it for the right to represent the workers in the plant: one possibility is at the anniversary of the certification, another is in the period leading up to the expiry of a contract.

In 1984 Manitoba labour law stated that a union could ask the Manitoba Labour Board to hold a certification vote if over 45 per cent of the potential members had signed union cards in the previous six months. Once the application was filed the employer was obliged to provide the union with a full list of the workforce. When Mitic got that list from the Labour Board he realized that Versatile had gone on a hiring binge—it was, he thought, unlikely that the union could reach the 45 per cent mark before the signed cards started to expire. With the union only a handful of cards short, Mitic considered going to the Labour Board and pleading for a vote. But this step, he concluded, would be a sign of weakness, and he chose simply to withdraw the application and begin the process again. At a meeting of the key organizers, he told the organizing committee, "We just missed by fifteen cards." Later he admitted that had pulled the number fifteen out of the air. "We weren't exactly sure how many it was, but I thought fifteen would help us and set the stage for the next campaign." Mitic committed the union to working for a vote in the spring of 1985, three months before the HEWA contract was due to expire on September 30, 1985.

Before that campaign got underway, though, the Canadian division of the UAW had undergone a major transformation. The recession of the early 1980s had a negative impact on the automobile market, leading to widespread layoffs and threats of plant closures. While the general UAW response to hard times was to reopen contracts and provide employers with concessions, the Canadian district took a more militant approach. In spring 1982 the Canadian UAW rejected a proposal to reopen the Ford and General Motors contracts. In the following year the Canadian workers won a bitter strike with Chrysler, setting the stage for a confrontation with GM in 1984. In the United States, the UAW settled with GM for a minimal wage increase, but the Canadian GM workers chose to strike for a share of the increase in the corporation's productivity. Following a thirteen-day strike, the Canadian workers won what was termed the "special Canadian adjustment." The victory heightened the growing tensions between the union's Canadian and U.S. leaders. It was becoming clear that if the UAW did not grant the Canadian division considerable autonomy, the Canadians were going to separate.

To force the issue Bob White and the rest of the union's Canadian leaders sought autonomy provisions that would guarantee that the Canadian division set the Canadian bargaining agenda, determine when strikes took place, and have access to the UAW strike fund. As the Canadian leaders expected, the UAW's international executive rejected the proposal, and on December 11, 1984, the UAW's Canadian council voted overwhelmingly to establish a new, all-Canadian union. At the time White wrote to the union members: "It is not a declaration of war on the companies we work for, on the American workers, or on the U.S. leadership of the International union. It is taking control of our own decisions, being accountable and responsible, and not passing the blame on to someone else." Following negotiations with the UAW, $36 million was transferred to the new union, which was to be known as the Canadian Auto Workers (CAW). At a convention in September 1985 White was elected as the union's first president.[15] It was a historic step, one that led not only to a number of other industrial unions gaining more autonomy from their international unions but also to a series of large-scale mergers within the Canadian labour movement. In short order the CAW, for example, was representing airline workers, fish-plant workers, and railway employees.

The creation of the CAW had little immediate impact on the organiz- ing campaign at Versatile, other than generating a little confusion around the name change. One night soon after the change took place Farrow found himself on a worker's doorstep where he introduced himself as Barrie Farrow of the CAW. The man looked at him and said, "What's that? Catholics Around the World?" Setting such oddities aside, Farrow said that the second drive was a dream. The organizing commit- tee was large, committed, and well prepared; and people who had held back the last time around were now coming to the union. Farrow laughed when he recalled how some people came into their own during the course of the drive. "There was one older guy, I thought the pen was going to fall out of his hand when he signed the union card. And three months later, on voting date, he's running around sticking stickers up throughout the plant. He just came out of his shell."

The union's success was due to a growing dissatisfaction with HEWA plus heightened concern over the company's future. As Cornat tottered on the edge of bankruptcy, the workers realized that they needed to have an organization with resources on their side. The movement to the CAW continued right to the last minute. The night before the CAW applied for the vote, when Farrow went to the plant gate, a worker met him and passed him a package of cigarettes. In it were some more signed union cards.

One of the first issues the Labour Board had to establish in the

Versatile case concerned just who would be allowed to vote. In the Labour Board hearing to determine the size of the bargaining unit, the company took the position that people on layoff should not be allowed to vote because they did not have a community of interest with the workers in the plant. The union took the position that many of the laid-off workers had been with the company for decades and been laid off many times. One of the union's key witnesses was Peter Magda, who outlined the number of times he had been laid off and recalled. According to Farrow, it was Magda's evidence that led the board to rule in the union's favour.

When the vote was held in the plant in July 1985, CAW supporter Jesse Esquera sat and watched the results being neatly placed in piles. At one point Esquera turned to Farrow and showed him a piece of foolscap on which he had scribbled his prediction: a CAW victory. A few moments later the prediction was confirmed when an angry Versatile official brushed a stack of ballots to the floor. A new era was about to begin at Versatile, and it would begin as it would end, with a conflict.

4

Building a Local

1985–2000

The Manitoba Labour Board granted the CAW a certificate to represent the production workers at Versatile on July 18, 1985. The members of the newly created Local 2224 elected Peter Magda as president and Len Rausch as the chairperson of the plant committee. The two men were to face difficult issues in the coming months.

By the end of September 1985 the company intended to lay off 760 of the 1,200 workers it had at the start of the year. It also wanted the union to present its bargaining proposals as soon as possible. When the union said it would not be ready to start bargaining until September 30, the company responded that it might not be prepared to operate without an agreement after that date. Versatile was, in effect, threatening to lock the workers out. Then, two days after talks started on September 30, company manager Lorne Blue told the union bargaining team that they would have to accept a 15 per cent wage cut. Hemi Mitic, now with the CAW, said the union would only consider such a measure after it had the opportunity to examine Versatile's books. Blue, refusing this request, announced that if the union did not accept the wage cut, the workers would be locked out at midnight on October 4. Mitic, not quite believing what he was hearing, told Blue, "You'd better not lock us out, it's going to be against the law. It's a violation of the labour relations act." The company declined Mitic's free legal advice, and the talks broke off.

Mitic immediately got in touch with Mel Myers, the union's Winnipeg legal counsel, and together they began developing a strategy. Both men were familiar with the labour code, which had been amended by the province's ruling New Democratic Party in the early 1980s. At the time the labour movement had been calling on the government to bring in laws that would prohibit the use of strikebreakers. While the NDP had adopted a policy that would have outlawed strikebreakers at its convention in 1980, party officials worried that the promise could be used against it in the 1981 election. As a result, NDP leader Howard Pawley made a public commitment that the party would not bring in anti-strikebreaking laws. Instead it promised to bring in a series of measures that would improve labour relations and reduce the likelihood of strikes in which employers made use of strikebreakers.

The NDP won the 1981 election and in 1982 the Pawley government brought in legislation prohibiting lockouts and any changes in wages or working conditions for the first ninety days after a union had been certified. At the request of the union or the employer, the Labour Board could further extend this ninety-day freeze. The logic behind this provision was that many bitter strikes and lockouts—often involving strikebreakers—took place over first contracts. In these conflicts, which were usually carryovers of failed attempts to keep the union from being certified, employers attempted to break unions by locking people out or cutting wages and benefits before new contracts could be negotiated. A number of employers had successfully employed these tactics to alienate workers from their unions and delay the negotiation of contracts until such a time when the workers simply voted to get rid of the unions. The new first-contract law prohibited all of these manoeuvres.

Mitic and Myers soon became convinced that the promised Versatile lockout was a textbook example of the sort of confrontation that the first contract was intended to eliminate, and they warned the company and its lawyers that if they went ahead and locked the union out, the union would bring them up on charges before the Labour Board. The company took the position that first-contract law did not apply in this situation because the CAW had inherited the HEWA contract. On October 4 it locked the workers out.

While Myers and Mitic were preparing the legal arguments, the bargaining committee had to transform itself into a strike committee. If the Versatile managers had thought the lockout would alienate the members from the union, they were in for a shock. According to Rausch, the older workers were outraged by the proposed wage cut and the lockout. "They were on the picket line yelling and screaming, and it was the younger workers sort of hanging back." Rausch remembered company president Paul Soubry arriving in a BMW, and how the "old guys tore it apart." The anger was compounded by Versatile's announcement of a reduction in the workforce to seventy-five people. If the workers had been laid off before the lockout, they would have been eligible for unemployment insurance benefits. Now that they were locked out, they were not eligible for those benefits.

At the Labour Board, Mitic argued that Versatile had intended to simply go through the motions of bargaining until September 30, when, the company believed, it would have the legal right to lock the workers out. On October 22 the Board ruled that the company had committed an unfair labour practice. Two days later Blue told Mitic that the company did not intend on ending the lockout. Instead it appealed the decision and continued with the lockout until a contract was reached on November 9. The Board continued to rule in the favour of the union and ordered Versatile to pay the workers the $794,532 in pay and $188,209 in unemployment insurance benefits that they had lost as a result of the lockout. Myers recalled the record-setting victory: "It was wonderful, one of the best things I ever did in terms of the law and also in terms of the results for people." The company appealed the Labour Board decision to the Court of Queen's Bench, arguing that the Board had overstepped its authority. It was not until the spring of 1986 that the Court upheld the Labour Board ruling.

Shortly after the Court had ordered Versatile to compensate its locked-out workers for lost wages, Myers registered the judgment and placed a lien against the Versatile property. In the end this move appeared to be a stroke of genius. In 1987, when the company was being sold to Ford New Holland, Versatile had still not paid the Labour Board award to the Winnipeg workers. Because the union had filed the lien, it was in a position to block the deal. For a while it looked as if a $180-million deal might be scuttled by a million dollar debt. Once Ford realized that the lien had to be paid off before the purchase could go ahead, the company phoned CAW president Bob White and offered the union thirty-three cents on the dollar. White passed the message on to Rausch, who told him to turn it down. Some twenty minutes later White phoned back, saying the company was up to sixty-six cents on the dollar. Rausch said, "Bob, you didn't hear me the first time. I said, 'It's all or shut the goddamn doors.'" Ford paid up in full, the workers finally got their lost wages, and the sale went through.

The year 1988 was to be a breakthrough time for the CAW at Versatile, with the union winning dramatic improvements to wages and benefits. But the talks did not start well. At the table the company was pleading poverty, claiming that its labour costs were close to 25 per cent of the cost of each tractor; without a wage rollback the company might even have to shut the plant down. Rausch could see that Versatile's constant barrage was wearing down the other members of the bargaining committee. Then he received a phone call from a friend in management, who told him that he had computer printouts on his desk that the union might find interesting. The friend said he was going out for coffee and would not be upset to discover on his return that the documents were gone. Rausch dropped into the office and scooped up the huge pile of documents. At a glance the hundreds of pages appeared to be nothing more than detailed measurements of the costs of various tractor components. But the last page included a summary that showed the cost of labour for each tractor line. According to Versatile's documents, the labour costs on tractors were between 3.8 and 7.9 per cent of the total costs, depending on the make of the tractor.

Rausch knew that compared to John Deere and Case, the Versatile wages were extremely low. "Our tractors sold at the same price as theirs, but they were making $30-some an hour U.S. and we were making $12 Canadian at that time." Because of the secretive way in which the information had come to him, he decided not to share it with the other bargaining committee members at the time. He did show the sheets to CAW staff representative Ron Joyal, who suggested that they take the document to the union's pension expert, Sym Gill, who confirmed Rausch's interpretation. Wages were not a problem at Versatile. At this point Rausch shared the information with the committee members, who were greatly relieved. Rausch made a photocopy of the document, being careful to leave off the dates on which it had been printed, thereby making it impossible for the company to identify who had leaked the documents.

At the next bargaining session Rausch and Joyal asked the company's chief negotiator to meet with them in the hallway. Rausch said, "You know I've been out of school for twenty-two years, but I just can't figure out how you get this 25 per cent labour cost." He pulled the photocopy out of his back pocket and gave it to the negotiators, who looked at it and said, "Where did you get this?" Rausch said, "Yeah, right, I'm going to tell you." The negotiator turned around, looked at the document some more, and said, "Fuck." And, Rausch said later, "He was a religious guy, never swore, never drank, nothing. It sort of rattled him a bit." Rausch said that he and Joyal had conducted the conversation away from the bargaining table because they did not want to belittle the company negotiator in front of his own team. It was the last they would hear about high labour costs in those talks.

The momentum was now with the union. Joyal argued that the Versatile workers were now Ford workers and should get what other Ford workers received. The 1988 contract, approved by 583 union members, included a wage increase that for some workers amounted to 23 per cent over three years; a supplementary unemployment insurance benefit that would see the company top-up unemployment insurance benefits for laid-off workers by $100 a week, bringing total weekly earnings for laid-off workers to $440; and a continuation of medical benefits for the first twenty-six weeks of any layoff. An improved pension plan provided most pensioners with an additional $90 a month, although some would see increases of up to $140. In a first for any union in Manitoba, the contract contained a provision for a member-sponsored fund to pay legal fees for divorces, real estate transactions, and wills.[1]

The legal-fee provision got considerable attention, but for the Versatile workers themselves a new seniority provision was one of the most important elements in the contract. Critics see seniority provisions as measures that protect less skilled workers and prevent the employer from promoting only the most skilled or ambitious workers. Seniority clauses do limit management's ability to make promotions or layoffs on a unilateral basis, but then employers do not always make promotion or layoff decisions solely on the basis of ability. The Versatile workers knew this first-hand—people who were too independent, from the wrong ethnic or religious group, or perhaps just too old often believed that they had been passed over by management. Seniority is one of the few contract provisions that recognizes what is usually overlooked in North American labour relations—namely, that workers invest more than their labour in a job, they also invest their lives. Forty-year-old workers will never get their twenties and thirties back; they will never be able to build up a lengthy employment history with another company. The limited job security that seniority provides is simply a well-earned return on their investment. As well, in North America management generally refuses to bargain over the quality of work. Under their management rights provisions, employers seek to retain the right to determine what should be made and how it should be made. Often the only hope for workers who have been given dirty, dangerous, and difficult jobs is the prospect of eventually using their seniority to bid on easier jobs and shifts.[2]

Under many seniority schemes employers identify the workers who are to be laid off. These workers then have the option of bumping into the job of a worker who has less seniority. Employers generally seek to have as many restrictions as possible on these bumping rights. They might require, for example, that when bumping, workers can't move into a different job classification than one they are already in, or that they have demonstrated that they have the skills to do the job that they are seeking to bump into. In these situations, although workers have bumping rights, there is often no job they can move into. Unions prefer to have plant-wide seniority provisions, which allow laid-off workers to bump into any job for which they can be trained. This was the type of seniority provision that the CAW bargained at Versatile.

As Scott McLaren put it, "Under the CAW seniority provisions the company was supposed to train the most senior person up to the job." When the company tried to move to a situation in which skill and ability would have an impact on the seniority decision, the union put its foot down, arguing that the company's "skill and ability tests were just too one-sided," that the union couldn't trust the company to do the right thing. The other side of it, McLaren said, was that if workers were found not to be doing the job required, the union would work with the company to find an alternative. "We watched it carefully," McLaren said. "If we saw people who were putting their names up that we knew couldn't do the job, we would speak to them." If there was a problem with someone doing a particular job, they would pull a guy to the side and say, "Look, you know you're not making it here."

Sometimes this way of doing things got the union "in hot water"—sometimes the union "took it on the chin" from its members for doing that. "But at Versatile we always prided ourselves on the fact that if the company came to us and could show us a legitimate problem, we'd deal with it," McLaren said. "We didn't live in a vacuum like a lot of unions do." The company was always trying to take away the seniority provisions and the key, according to McLaren, was to deal with issues identified by management as those issues came up, rather than having to deal with them in the bargaining sessions when the union wanted to focus instead on getting a better pension, better wages, better working conditions.

Paul Lussier's work history underlines the degree to which the Versatile workers valued their seniority benefits. When he was laid off in 1991 Lussier went to work at New Flyer Industries, a bus-manufacturing plant. When his recall came nine months later he considered staying with New Flyer. He liked the work there, but in the end decided that he did not want to give up the seniority he had built up at Versatile. Jaime De La Rosa had a similar experience. He was laid off, got another decent job, and eventually went back to Versatile because he did not want to lose his seniority, which dated back to 1979. The Versatile layoffs could be lengthy, and to further protect its members' seniority rights the union negotiated a forty-eight-month recall period into the contract. This provision meant that in the event of a plant closure, workers who had been laid off for up to four years would be eligible for severance pay.

The CAW's model in its negotiations with Ford New Holland was its contracts with the Ford Motor Company. While the Versatile workers never achieved the sort of wages and benefits that characterize CAW contracts with the Big Three auto manufacturers, the union made numerous gains through its approach of arguing that the Versatile workers were Ford employees and deserved the same treatment as other Ford employees.

Economists categorize companies like Ford as firms that operate in the core sector of the economy as opposed to operating on the periphery. The core-sector firms, generally large multinational corporations, have few competitors, rarely go bankrupt, and can exercise control not only over the competitive companies that supply them but also over the markets for their products. They usually have very large investments in plants and machinery, which means that labour is a relatively small portion of their overall costs. As a result wages and benefits at core firms are generally better than in the peripheral firms, which exist in a much more competitive atmosphere, invest less in technology, and make greater use of labour. Where core firms have generally learned to live with unions, anti-union sentiment is much higher among employers on the periphery. The peripheral firms put up strong fights to keep unions out and are prepared to force a strike in an effort to break an existing union.

From the workers' perspective the Ford New Holland takeover represented a significant improvement. Unlike Cornat, Ford was not interested in stripping every last penny of value out of the company. The owner carried out long-delayed improvements and cleaned up and renovated the plant. Ford's experience with the CAW and UAW in other plants meant that the company and the union were talking the same language. But, more ominously, the Ford purchase also signalled the end of Versatile's versatility as a number of product lines were dropped. The swathers, for example, were now to be manufactured by MacDon, a small non-union Winnipeg implement firm. The company also began an increasing drive to contract out work, which meant the elimination of jobs—a process that in turn makes it easier for a company to shut down production in an assembly plant, packing up the equipment and opening up shop in another country. At Versatile the welding and tool-and-dye shops were gradually downsized. In a union newsletter in 1998 Rausch and McLaren outlined the extent of the downsizing that had taken place since the plant's purchase by New Holland: "In 1984 we had in the bargaining unit approximately 185 welders whereas today we only have 60. Department 520 employed 95 sheet metal workers, today there are

5. Machine Shop had over 100 employees and now has 15."[3] While the union won a number of grievances about the contracting out of work, it was not able to reverse the trend.

During the 1980s the CAW grew dramatically both in Manitoba and across Canada. While the autoworker name inevitably conjures up images of assembly-line workers turning out this year's model for one of the Big Three auto companies in Ontario's Golden Triangle, a series of mergers in the late 1980s and early 1990s led to both a big jump in CAW membership and a change in the composition of that membership. In Manitoba the union membership came to include skilled craft workers on the CN and CP railways, steel-mill employees at Griffin Steel, maintenance workers at the University of Manitoba, call-centre workers at Air Canada, production workers at the Bristol and Boeing aircraft plants and New Flyer bus plant, dairy workers at Parmalat Dairies, warehouse workers at TrueServ Hardware, and cooks and cleaning personnel at the Fort Garry Hotel.

In 1991 the union appointed Dale Paterson as the Area Director for Manitoba, Saskatchewan, and the Northwest Territories. Paterson got his start in the labour movement as a Pacific Western Airlines ramp attendant in 1973. As he put it, his union career is like an age-old story. He thought the union, then the Canadian Airline Employees Association, had not done a proper job of representing a co-worker. He raised the issue and the next thing he knew he was a union steward. By the late 1970s he was working in Castlegar, B.C., where he helped co-ordinate the union's 1978 strike. He and other members of his Local were fired for refusing to cross another union's picket line. In 1984 he went on staff with the union, which merged with the Auto Workers the following year. Before his appointment to the Winnipeg office Paterson worked in Calgary and Halifax.

The rich political culture of the Versatile Local made a strong impression on Paterson. The union had at least three different if informal political groupings. One group, taking its leadership from workers associated with the old Association, generally favoured a more conciliatory approach to management. A second group, which dominated the union, was led by people who were seen to be supporters of the New Democratic Party. These included Len Rausch, who was the plant chairperson from 1985 to 1994. The third group was led by people who were associated with a number of smaller left-wing parties, although at times its leadership was provided by NDP supporter Peter Magda, who served as the union's president from 1985 to 1988 and again from 1994 to 1997. While members might shift their support from one group to another, the divisions between the factions could be intense at times. Even though Rausch and Magda were both New Democrats they were often at loggerheads with one another, indicating that the differences were often not based on simple partisan politics. The knock against Rausch was that he was prone to behind-the-scenes discussions with management. Magda was seen as someone who would take the company on in a head-on fashion, but he would also take on his fellow union members in the same way. His rough-and-ready approach alienated some union members.

Another leading figure in the union, Sandy Brar, came to Canada with a strong grounding in radical politics. Many of Brar's family members and friends had been active in the highly militant Indian Communist Party. Radical politics, he said, came "from the home, from friends, and college." Brar served as a shop steward and chairperson of the human rights committee and spent three terms as financial secretary of the union. With a number of Chileans, he helped established a strong left-wing caucus at Versatile. The caucus also included Magda, Winston Johnson, and Paul Lussier, among others—people who, Brar said, were not communists in any sense, but militants. According to Lussier, Brar was "soft-spoken" but "forceful" when he had to be. "I learned a lot from him."

Lussier was at times angered when opponents tried to discredit the views of the left caucus because some of the members belonged to various communist parties. "It was like McCarthyism, with people claiming that there's one under every bed and, well, we've got to watch these guys and that.... So that can hurt you going to the table. The company looks at it and goes, 'These guys are really divided.' When you're divided you're too busy fighting one another instead of fighting the company." On the contrary, Lussier said, "these guys" they talked about were "no different from me or you." According to Lussier the internal disputes never played themselves out during negotiations. While he and Rausch rarely saw eye to eye, during negotiations they backed each other up. "You just can't play these games out during the course of negotiations." For his part, Paterson recalled that he often had to impose a temporary truce on the various factions at the start of negotiations.

> I remember having a couple of meetings with a couple of bargaining committees and saying we've got to put the politics aside because we're trying to get a collective agreement for everybody. We've even put out bulletins that I made them all sign, saying there's a truce, you know, during this round of

bargaining. As soon as the bargaining was done, man, they would go back and the politics would be stirred up again.

As fractious as it sounds, Paterson said the political conflicts drove the union in a positive direction. "If we needed something done by workers, we could call on the Versatile guys and they'd be there."

Not surprisingly Louis Mora became involved in politics at Versatile. But while the Chilean refugee remained a person of the left, he did not participate in any of the caucuses. "I was very outspoken. I am not a person who you can tell what to do or think," he said. "If I am convinced that what you are telling me is right, I will fight for that with everything that I have. But if I am not, I won't do it. I cannot convince other people if I cannot convince myself." As a result Mora sometimes found himself on the outs with both the NDP caucus, even though he was a New Democrat, and the left caucus. He had harsh words about all the Versatile caucuses. They used politics in the "wrong way," he thought. The smearing, the backstabbing, is not political. Politics for me is the art of government." Despite his unwillingness to join a caucus, he was able to get elected to the bargaining committee for eight years. While on the committee he was one of the main advocates of a severance plan—a payout made to employees in the event of a plant closure. During negotiations management had rejected the proposal, saying the plant's future was secure. Mora said if that was the case, the severance package would not cost the company anything—an argument that, to Mora's surprise, prevailed.

Mora also served as Scott McLaren's political and union mentor, though McLaren's initial involvement in the CAW was sparked not by ideology, but by unhappiness about how a co-worker had been treated. McLaren believed that the union had not done enough when a friend of his was fired. He spoke up about the union's failings, and the next thing he knew he had been elected as the stores department's representative on the union bargaining committee. While he worked hard not to be identified with any of the caucuses, he became active in the NDP. Both he and Rausch were active in the Concordia NDP riding association and were supporters of Gary Doer, who made the jump from the Manitoba Government Employees' Association to provincial politics when he successfully ran for the NDP nomination in Concordia in 1986. Two years later Doer became NDP leader.

McLaren soon came to believe that the existence of different political factions made for a stronger union. "You couldn't just go out there and just hold up your hand and say 'pick me.' You had to know the issues, you had to be out there, you had to be very knowledgeable to get elected. It was not an easy task to be elected at Versatile. Sometimes we'd be running eight or nine people for the same position." Winston Johnson echoed those views. "If you were a candidate you were challenged. People looked at your educational background, what courses you had taken." It was "big-time politics," Johnson said. "People were really running on their records and anything that you have done or you have said at a meeting might be used against you." A CAW staff representative once told Johnson that with Local 2224, the union had created a monster. "There were so many guys that were educated and politically motivated," Johnson said, "and we would all challenge the staff reps. And if I didn't like an answer I got from a staff rep or my area director I could take it to the national president. The structure's designed that way. They're prepared to give you a hearing and that's what I like about CAW structure."

The Local's members had a number of good reasons for contesting the elected positions beyond their commitment to the union. The CAW constitution provides for the election of both a union executive, which is headed by the president of the Local, and a plant committee, which is headed by the plant chairperson. The president and the executive are responsible for the union's finances, its relations with the national union and the provincial labour movement, and its political, social, and educational services. The nine-member plant committee bargains and polices the collective agreement. The chair of the committee has an office in the plant and works full-time on union issues while being paid by the company, while the Local president is paid by the company to work one day a week on union business. Some committee and executive members are granted what is known as preferential or super seniority—in other words, they cannot be laid off, even if they do not have as much seniority as workers who are being laid off. Super seniority prevents the company from targeting union activists and also provides for continuity of union leadership. The plant committee members were also to be paid for hours lost when they attended bargaining sessions.

There was much more to the Local than its wages and benefits. Johnson was particularly impressed with the CAW's internal education program. The union, he said, was continuously working at educating its membership, running programs throughout the year at places like the Union Centre on Broadway in Winnipeg or at Port Elgin in Ontario. Johnson himself attended weekend schools and shop steward training sessions, went through bargaining committee training, and attended workshops on human rights. To Brar the CAW was a family experience.

At various times he, his wife, and his two children all went to the CAW's educational centre in Port Elgin. The union had organized the plant where his wife worked. When she was forced out of that workplace as the result of her union activity, CAW staff representative Cecille Cassista helped her find another job.

Brar talked with pride about Local 2224's militancy. When striking workers at other Winnipeg plants had sent letters asking for money, the Local would not only send a cheque, but also send members down to bolster the picket lines. It was also militant in its dealings with the employer. In 1994 the Local went on strike for nine days, winning a three-year contract that included improvements to the pension plan, a 7 per cent pay increase plus a cost-of-living adjustment, and a wage-security plan that topped unemployment insurance benefits when workers were on layoff. At the time Paterson said that the agreement should show employers that "the wage-freeze mentality for workers" was over.[4] Looking back on the strike, Paterson said he suspected the company was in large measure testing the union members in that conflict, forcing them into a strike to see how serious the union was.

As a result of all this activity, by the end of the 1990s many of the workers were feeling somewhat satisfied. Stan Letwyn thought, "It had taken us a lot of years to get what we wanted, but it was not a bad place to work. There were a couple of problems, but we had a relatively clean shop." The workers had a union that protected them, the wages were relatively good for Manitoba, and Letwyn was looking forward to retirement from the plant." For others the friendships formed at Versatile had become an essential part of life. "I liked working there," John Pfeiffer said. "I enjoyed going to work. There were a good bunch of guys, a good bunch of co-workers." Ed Balik agreed: "It had been a good company. Good wages, benefits and a good atmosphere."

The company was not standing still. In 1998 it came out with its latest bidirectional tractor, the TV140. Larger and more powerful than the previous bidirectional models, it was heralded as the company's entry into newer markets. In the late 1990s, under Fiat ownership, senior company executives came to Manitoba to speak with CAW officials about a possible $110-million investment in the plant. The company appeared to be interested in trading the investment for contract concessions, but the discussions did not reach the point at which Fiat would make any commitments.

At one point the Fiat officials explained to Paterson that the company was likely to take a tough position in bargaining with the union. Paterson answered, "Well, we're tough too." They both agreed they were tough, Paterson said, and "nothing happened." Lussier believed that Fiat wanted to weaken seniority rights. There was "no way," he thought at the time, "that this union would ever buy into that, never happen, not in a million years. They even tried to buy off the bargaining committee. They wanted to fly us all down to Italy to show us how this works. We wouldn't buy into it, it just wasn't happening."

After those discussions the Winnipeg plant appeared to fall off the Fiat radar screen. Although no new investments were forthcoming, the plant remained profitable despite being subject to the fluctuations of the agricultural economy. The union was secure in the belief that it made a good product and Fiat had no interest in getting out of the tractor business. What the members did not foresee was the possibility of Fiat purchasing another tractor firm.

5

The Merger and Its Fallout

1999–2000

May 1999: a news release announces the merger of J.I. Case and the Fiat-owned New Holland.

It was a sign of the evolution of the North American farm implement industry that the news release announcing the merger of these two companies, both founded in the United States, was issued by a man named Jean-Pierre Rosso from an office in Amsterdam. According to Rosso, the president of Case, the $4.3-billion transaction would create a new $12-billion company, Case New Holland, with Fiat holding a controlling interest. As U.S. financial analyst Eli Lustgarten said, "You have an Italian-run company, chartered in the Netherlands, based in London, being turned around and run by an American company headed by a Frenchman."[1]

The size of the two firms was staggering: in 1998 Fiat had recorded revenues of $56.6 billion, Case of $6.1 billion. Rosso boasted:

> We are creating a new company with an extraordinary range of products and services that will meet the needs of more customers around the world than any other equipment company, while also capturing the significant synergies of a company of this scale and scope. Through our combined resources and strengths, we will have the capabilities to lead the technological changes and emerging market opportunity that are developing through out industry today.

Rosso promised shareholders that the merger would save between $400 million and $500 million within three to four years.[2]

The news left anyone watching the event closely with two questions on their minds. First, would the U.S. Justice Department approve the creation of such an industry giant? Second, if it did, which of the new company's thirty-nine plants would be shut down to come up with the promised half-billion dollars in savings?

Dale Paterson had a sick feeling that he knew the answer to the second question. There was good reason to worry about New Holland's Versatile plant. In response to a dramatic decline in demand for tractors, the plant had been in semi-shutdown since September 1998. Although Rosso was saying that New Holland and Case did not have overlapping product lines, Peterson was well aware that Case had tractor plants in Racine, Wisconsin, and Fargo, North Dakota, that were operating at less than full capacity. He immediately asked for a meeting with New Holland's senior managers. CAW national president Buzz Hargrove wrote to both the federal and provincial governments, urging them to take steps to protect the Winnipeg plant. He also argued, "The incredible cost competitiveness of Canadian manufacturing operations, based on lower labour costs, our socialized health care system, and high productivity, should strengthen the argument in favour of maintaining or even expanding New Holland production at Winnipeg."[3] Hargrove made it clear that he expected the provincial government not to stand by while production moved elsewhere. In a letter to Conservative Premier Gary Filmon, Hargrove wrote:

> Keep in mind that the US states which will also be competing for investment from the new company have been extremely aggressive in recent years with location subsidies and other incentives. All the jargon in the world about the problems associated with this type of practice cannot justify a hands-off approach by Canadian governments, if that approach contributes to the loss of productive Canadian jobs.[4]

The argument alluded to the concerns that many, on all ends of the political spectrum, have raised when regional governments make concessions to attract investment.

The union's pitch was straightforward. If the plant was at full capacity, some eight hundred unionized workers would be making an average of $20 an hour turning out $6 million worth of product a day, most of it bound for export markets. Even during a period of extensive shutdown, the plant was putting out $3 million worth of product each day. The plant had the potential to become the new company's world production centre for large four-wheel-drive and bidirectional tractors. Since Case was in the process of shutting its one Canadian operation, located in Hamilton, closure of the Winnipeg plant would leave Case

New Holland with no Canadian presence. Finally, the plant was making tractors that had been designed with the support of the Canadian government. Symbolically, its presence demonstrated that Manitoba was a major presence in the agricultural implement manufacturing sector.

The CAW put together a working group aimed at keeping the plant in Winnipeg, even inviting the local plant management to participate in the committee. It also held meetings with representatives of the Winnipeg and Manitoba governments. A Manitoba government official told the media that the province had been in touch with the Fiat head office in Turin to press the case for the Winnipeg plant. While the various levels of government participated in the working group, the company declined to be involved. One news story suggested that the Case plant in Fargo had the edge over the Versatile plant because it produced a larger proportion of its own parts. This was bitter—and ironic—news in Winnipeg, where the union had long opposed the trend towards outsourcing at Versatile.[5]

The Versatile workers themselves had differing thoughts as to the meaning of the merger. Machinist Ed Balik said, "When I heard about the merger I could smell something bad coming." Ray Wilkie had seen too many ups and downs to panic. "We made a good product, and the company made money making it. It was not the first time Versatile had been down. We always survived. I believed we would survive this one too." Richard Ullmann, a machinist who had been with the company since 1979, knew there were would be problems as a result of the merger because the two companies had so many similar product lines, but still because of all the improvements that had been made around the plant, he didn't think it would be closed down. "The company had been spending quite a bit of money there. For example, a lot of money had been spent on developing the new Genesis tractor." Ullmann had good reason to be uneasy about the future. For twenty years his wife Sherry had worked in sales at the Eaton's store at Winnipeg's Polo Park mall. In October 1999 the store, along with most other Eaton's locations across the country, closed its doors. As Sherry recalled, "I was pretty upset, worrying about where we were going to get the money we needed. I moped around the house. There was no severance when the company went out of business. I went through quite a bit of rigmarole getting a little bit of money from EI and the liquidator."

In the provincial legislature NDP leader Gary Doer pressed Filmon on whether he intended to meet with the union to discuss the plant's future. The premier responded that he doubted he would have the time, but he expected that provincial Industry Minister Merv Tweed would meet with the workers. When Paterson and CAW representatives met with both Tweed and Winnipeg mayor Glen Murray that summer they stressed that as many as 2,400 direct and indirect Manitoba jobs were at stake.

It was clear that the U.S. government would put some sort of restrictions on the merger. The U.S. Justice Department took the position that as originally proposed the merger would substantially reduce competition in the manufacture and sale of four-wheel-drive tractors, large two-wheel-drive tractors, small square balers, large square balers, and self-propelled hay and forage equipment in the United States and Canada. Only two companies in Canada and the United States sold four-wheel-drive and large two-wheel-drive tractors. In 1998 Case had 27 per cent of the four-wheel-drive market and 25 per cent of the large two-wheel-drive market. Fiat, through New Holland, had 13 per cent of the four-wheel-drive market and 10 per cent of the two-wheel-drive market.

In early November 1999 the Department of Justice, after discussions with both companies, ruled that the merger could proceed if New Holland sold off its Genesis line of two-wheel-drive tractors, its Versatile line of four-wheel-drive tractors, and its tracked tractors, then in development. By singling out the Genesis and Versatile lines, the Justice Department was essentially requiring that New Holland sell the Winnipeg plant. Case would be obliged to sell its ownership interest in a hay and forage equipment operation in Hesston, Kansas. (This was the remnant of the Hesston Corporation, which had sought to buy Versatile in 1975.) The ruling concluded that without these concessions Case and Fiat would control a significant portion of the market, leading to an increase in prices, a reduction in quality, and a decrease in innovation. Case and New Holland were given 150 days to make the sales. If they failed to meet the deadline, the U.S. government could appoint a trustee to make the sales; in all likelihood the trustee would simply auction off the unsold divisions. Until the sales were made, the units had to be maintained as viable ongoing concerns.

At the same time that the ruling was released New Holland announced that it would be moving production of New Holland's TV140 bidirectional tractor to another facility within the merged company. The only good news for Winnipeg in the announcement was hearing that Case New Holland would have the right to buy tractors from the Versatile plant's new owner for a limited period of time.

As Scott McLaren told the *Winnipeg Free Press*, "We don't view this as a good thing. We like being in the New Holland family. Over the years we made a lot of money for New Holland and Fiat. It's disappointing that we were not looked at more favourably." McLaren said the union had been hoping that the "merger would be allowed to occur first and then we would have had a chance to make our case."[6] Many of the Versatile workers concluded that with a presidential election coming up in 2000, Justice Department officials had been prevailed upon to rule in favour of U.S. rather than Canadian jobs.

But who would buy the plant? There was little reason to think that the Department of Justice would look favourably on a sale to John Deere, one of the few established tractor manufacturers left standing. *Stark's News Service*, serving the truck and tractor industry, opined that Caterpillar, which was not in the tractor-manufacturing business at that time, might be interested in buying Versatile. The suggestion made sense because Caterpillar had a contract with New Holland to produce four-wheel-drive vehicles at the Winnipeg plant. The prospect of a Caterpillar takeover drew a mixed response from the CAW. The company had acquired a well-deserved reputation as a union buster: in 1991 it locked out the United Auto Workers at the start of what was to be a lengthy and punishing defeat that it inflicted on the union. But Caterpillar was also a multi-billion-dollar corporation. It had the resources and network to build and market tractors globally if it so chose.[7] AGCO was also interested, although union officials worried over that company's reputation for buying firms only to shut them down after gaining access to their customers and product lines. As recently as 1996 AGCO had bought and shut down Portage Manufacturing, a combine manufacturer in nearby Portage la Prairie.

Paterson responded to the ruling immediately, calling on newly elected NDP premier Gary Doer to convene a meeting with the Versatile management. Len Rausch and McLaren began to rev up a public campaign urging members to write to local politicians and to circulate petitions. The theme was simple: action had to be taken to make sure that the last tractor plant in Canada was not ploughed under.

Shortly after the Department of Justice announcement, Paterson was in Toronto attending a CAW national council meeting when a call came through to his hotel room. Craig Engel identified himself as an employee of John Buhler and said his boss was interested in buying Versatile. Engel said the Versatile operation would be a perfect fit for the Winnipeg-based entrepreneur, allowing him to bring a number of smaller, scattered operations under one roof. In the winter they could make tractors and in the summer prepare the company's winter line of products, such as snow blowers. Engel wanted to know if the union was interested in a private, off-the-record meeting. Paterson was interested—even though he knew a bit about John Buhler, and what he knew, he did not like. But he was used to dealing with employers he didn't like. "I thought this might not be a bad idea. It was a homegrown solution that could keep the plant viable and have the ownership here in Manitoba."

Paterson set up a confidential meeting with Engel. He, Rausch, McLaren, and Bob Chernecki, an assistant to Hargrove, would attend. Paterson wanted to keep the conversations with Buhler quiet until they were able to find out something about the implications of the Buhler proposal for the CAW members. If they liked the deal, they were prepared to lobby the government on the company's behalf.

John Buhler, at age sixty-seven, was something of a force of nature in the Winnipeg business community. Born and raised in Morden, Manitoba, Buhler had dropped out of school in Grade ten to work at a gas station. He decided to get into sales when he sold a used car to a friend for more than it was worth. As he told business writer Judy Waytiuk, "I shouldn't have sold that car to him. But he wanted it. And that was when I knew I could sell." Buhler later said that as a teenager he had developed two ambitions—to have over one hundred employees (an ambition that bloomed to reach one thousand) and to build tractors.

He worked as an assistant station manager for the Canadian Pacific Railway for four years and then, at age twenty-one, with a thousand dollars borrowed from his father and five hundred dollars of his own savings, opened a Rambler dealership in Morden. Along the way he started dating the daughter of Adolph Krushel, the wealthiest man in Morden. In 1933 Krushel had founded Standard Gas Engine, which manufactured farm equipment, including the highly successful Farm King grain grinder. When the company faltered in the late 1960s Buhler loaned Krushel, by then his father-in-law, some needed capital. In 1970 Buhler took over the company for $150,000, renaming it Farm King and later Buhler Industries. He dramatically increased its product line, making it Canada's largest manufacturer of snow blowers.[8]

One of Buhler's admirers, Michael Decter, played a leading role in three NDP administrations: he worked for Ed Schreyer's cabinet planning and priorities committee, served as clerk of the executive council in Howard Pawley's administration, and was deputy minister of health when Bob Rae was premier of Ontario. In his book, *Michael Decter's Million Dollar Strategy: Building Your Own Retirement Fund in Just Thirty Minutes a Day*, Decter tells about first encountering Buhler during his days with the Pawley government. "In 1984, he sought to buy the money-losing, government-owned Flyer Industries—for $1, if memory serves. While unsuccessful in this acquisition, Mr. Buhler has successfully purchased a number of businesses, including Dominion Lumber, Birchwood Furniture, and Ideal Glass and Mirror Makers." According to Decter, Buhler is often referred to as a bottom-feeder:

> This phrase sounds more negative than it should; a more positive way of depicting Mr. Buhler is as a value investor. His base, Allied Farm King, is a farm equipment manufacturer that makes not expensive combines in competition with John Deere and Ford, but smaller farm implements, which the vast majority of farmers can afford.[9]

One of Buhler's first turnarounds was Allied Farm Equipment, which he bought in 1981 for $2.5 million. Allied was the first Manitoba company to sign up for the federal government's work-sharing program, introduced in response to a fierce economic recession. Under this plan the employer paid its workers full wages for four days' work and 40 per cent of their wages for the fifth day. The government would pick up the remaining 60 per cent. Before the Versatile strike was over, Buhler would publicly rail about government interference in the economy, but he was not above accepting government assistance.

He enjoyed talking to reporters, showing off his small cluttered office, and boasting of his tireless work habits. When he was working on a takeover he got by on four hours' sleep, while the modest office was to encourage other executives not to put on airs. He liked to say that he tried to take a holiday once, but had not enjoyed it. As his chief operating officer Engel commented to the *Free Press*, "If it's Italian suits and $50 haircuts and one-and-a-half-hour lunches you're looking for, this isn't the place to work. He expects a lot out of his people but he expects even more from himself."[10]

Buhler never tired of expounding the virtues of what he called "Buhler logic," the prime rule of which was that one should break "all the rules they teach you in the commerce faculty." His own key rules were no consultants, pay in time to get a discount, and never lease. A manager might get by the first time he leased an item, but after the second time, Buhler explained, "I'd be helping him write his resume." In an era when the prevailing view was that businesses had to go global or die, Buhler focused almost solely on selling in what he termed his backyard—North America. Sales to the United States were not, in his opinion, export sales. Buhler Industries was listed on the Toronto Stock

Exchange, even though the owner claimed not to need additional capital. He did join the list, he said, partly out of vanity—to read his name in the paper every day.

The Buhler Industries headquarters was an unprepossessing old International Harvester warehouse in Transcona, a working-class suburb on Winnipeg's east side. From there Buhler oversaw five manufacturing plants with six distribution centres. Despite the at times chaotic diversification—a glass factory in Ontario, lawn and garden tools, food, furniture, poultry, steel fabrication, and real estate—farm implements such as front-end loaders and blades accounted for 75 per cent of Buhler Industries revenue in 1999. He also owned Amarillo Services, which operated a network of 1,400 dealers through which Buhler sold his implements.

Whether people saw him as a bottom-feeder or as "a saviour"—as fellow country-boy turned eccentric millionaire Bill Loewen described him—there could be little argument that the "Buhler logic" was successful. By the time he was putting in his bid on Versatile, Buhler could look back on thirty profitable years. In 1999 the *Globe and Mail Report on Business Magazine* placed Buhler Industries in its top 250 in terms of return on capital and return on equity. Annual sales were $65 million, profits were $4 million, and assets were valued at $61.1 million. But while Buhler Industries was successful, it was also an example of a company that operated on the economic periphery. Hundreds of other companies supplied products similar to Buhler's and his total empire was worth less than the Versatile plant and inventory. While one of his plants was unionized, wages and benefits were far lower than what the CAW workers earned at Versatile.

Buhler had already once tried to buy Versatile, in 1987, and he was in Ecuador when the U.S. Justice Department issued its November 1999 ruling. By mid-November he was back in Manitoba and had gone public with his intention to bid on the company. He pointed out that in the past Versatile had said he was too small to take over the company. "At that time, Versatile had 600 or 700 employers and I had about 200," he told a reporter. "Now I have 600 and there are only about 300 people working at Versatile."[11] Buhler said he would make the bid in conjunction with the German firm Weidemann GmbH and Co KG; Buhler distributed that company's industrial wheel loaders in North America. He said he intended in the end to build the wheel loaders at the Winnipeg plant. (As events unfolded, Weidemann was not part of the final deal.)

In the subculture of Winnipeg's industrial workers, Buhler did not enjoy the "aw shucks" country-boy image that seemed so prevalent in the business press. Over the years many Versatile employees had worked at Buhler's plants while they were on layoff, and many more of them had friends who worked for Buhler. He had a reputation for being a low-pay, weak-benefit patriarch. He could be tough to work for and tough to bargain with. On the one hand he had allowed employees to buy stock at preferred prices—an option that more than half his workforce had bought into—and the workers at one of his operations were unionized. On the other hand he was seen as a strict disciplinarian with no compunction about chewing people out. As one worker said, "If someone's caught with their feet up on their desk reading the comics at two in the afternoon, the whole office is going to hear about it." He was proud of underpaying his workforce—after all, he said, the workers were underpaid equally.[12]

"Buhler, his name meant to me that it would be nothing but trouble," Paul Lussier said. "I mean I know people that worked here for him, at Buhler on Regent, and he has total disregard for the working-class people in this province." Once when Jaime De La Rosa had been on layoff he had found work at one of Buhler's factories:

> The wages were not as good and there was always a threat of being fired. There was a bonus, but even if you work your ass off and make the bonus, the wages could not compete with what we made at Versatile. When there were negotiations he threatened to move the plant if the union did not give him what he wanted.

Over the twenty years that he worked for Versatile, Dwight Pitcher had been laid off on numerous occasions, taking jobs with firms such as New Flyer and Pauwels Canada, but he said it was only during his last layoff that he applied for a job at Buhler Industries. "This man had a reputation for thinking that fourteen bucks an hour is a good wage. No one wanted to work for him."

The CAW had its own limited experience with Buhler. In 1997 Buhler had purchased shares in Greensteel Industries, a steel fabrications company that was facing liquidation. As the company's chief share-holder, Buhler ended up dictating its bargaining position in contract negotiations with the CAW. In particular he insisted on a five-year agreement, while the CAW opposed lengthy agreements as a matter of policy. The union's policy preference for short-term contracts is based not only on the belief that long-term contracts make it impossible for the members to bargain improvements during periods of economic growth but also on a recognition of collective bargaining as one of the most significant activities for a Local. A Local that bargains once every five years is at risk of becoming weak and moribund. Paterson, who had not been involved in the Greensteel talks until that point, came to the table to see if he could help fashion an agreement that would be acceptable to the union. He arrived to find that Buhler was there, accompanied by a Winnipeg lawyer with extensive labour relations experience. Paterson knew the lawyer could be a tough negotiator, but he expected that with him at the table it might be possible to make progress in the talks. When the lawyer started to play a role in the discussion, Buhler cut him off, making it clear that he would handle the talks. In the end the Greensteel Local members decided that they had no choice but to accept the long-term agreement. This led to a rift between the Local and the CAW—with the workers choosing to leave the CAW.

Despite this history, Paterson was not prepared to write Buhler off. Every effort, he thought, had to be made to save the plant. Then he received a phone call from a reporter with *Starks News Service* asking questions about the upcoming meeting between the union and Buhler. Paterson declined comment and put through a call to the CAW's Chernecki, who denied having gone to the media with the story. The two men concluded that Buhler or Engel had put out the story in an effort to box the union into supporting his bid before it had time to analyze his proposal. A furious Paterson put in a call to Engel. "I blasted him for trying to waste us in public when this was meant to be a quiet behind-the-scenes meeting." From that day forward Buhler was at the bottom of the CAW's list of preferred purchasers.

In mid-November NDP Member of Parliament Pat Martin asked what the federal government was doing to help find a buyer. He also raised what was to prove to be a vexing question: what was the federal government doing to protect its loan to New Holland? Of the $45 million lent in 1987, $32 million still had to be repaid to the federal government. Ron Duhamel, the Liberal cabinet minister responsible for Western Economic Diversification, said he believed that New Holland was obligated to pay back the loan even if the plant closed. He still held out hope that a purchaser could be found. He also believed that, based on Versatile's recent repayment of another $5-million loan, the $32 million was not at risk.[13]

The CAW had been careful to cultivate the support of local politicians in its campaign to secure a buyer for Versatile. In January it sponsored a rally at the International Inn that was addressed by the premier, the mayor, and two members of parliament. Doer promised the workers: "We will drop anything at any time because this is a number one economic priority for us. Your plant and your future is our future. I am here to assure you of that today." For Doer, a major part of the commitment that he had made to the Versatile workers was to ensure that the loan would be made available to any new purchaser. To this end he spoke on several occasions with Duhamel and Industry Minister John Manley. Speaking about it in 2004, Doer said that his International Inn meeting commitment was to "fight as hard as I could to make sure that the loan provision would be there for a new buyer." With a half-grimace, half-smile, he added, "The thinking on that became a little different a couple of years later."

Mayor Glen Murray quickly surpassed Doer in enthusiasm, telling the workers:

> We are the best and the biggest in this because we have the plant and we have the best workforce. We're going to start building new partners as we did with New Flyer and get other investors. We're just simply not going to stop until we're the best, so let's not give up until we get there.

At the union's prompting Winnipeg City Council passed a motion to call on all levels of government to work together to secure the plant's future.

Starting in February 2000 Local vice-president Stan Letwyn and executive member John Pimental took the campaign to shopping centres with a toy tractor raffle and a postcard campaign to the federal and provincial governments to ask them to help find a buyer. The union also took out ads in the local newspapers urging Winnipeggers not to let the gates of the country's last tractor factory be closed. "It's time for action. Contact the Mayor, your MLA and MP to voice your concerns. Don't let Canadian jobs and an important part of our economy be ploughed under." The union reinforced the message on billboard space purchased throughout the city. Because Pimental had worked as an expediter he knew the names of the local firms that did business with Versatile. As a result he and Letwyn were able to obtain letters of support from most of the company's local suppliers. The union also successfully approached most of the businesses around the plant in search of support—restaurants, autobody shops, and hotels all reasoned that their businesses would suffer if the plant were closed.

The union was alarmed that New Holland appeared to be dragging its feet about looking for a buyer. It took the company two months from the Department of Justice ruling to put together a prospectus, a document that provides prospective buyers with the details of just what is for sale. Rausch and McLaren were also frustrated that the company declined to take part in the working group established by the union, severely limiting the group's effectiveness. The union was not easily able to find out who was interested in buying the plant. Otherwise, McLaren said, "It would have been a simple thing for us to go down and say to a company that we thought was viable, look we are prepared to do what it takes. We never got a chance to speak to the perspective buyers in that way."

At times McLaren and Rausch wondered if New Holland was not discouraging anyone who could make a go of it from buying the plant. McLaren said, "It looked to us as if New Holland thought it was better off selling it to someone who is not viable and would run it into the ground." Alternately they feared that the company would delay the sale to the point where the U.S. government would simply appoint a trustee to close the plant and sell off its product lines. The CAW reckoned that there were at least four potential buyers for the company. It also believed that as a condition of sale, the Winnipeg plant should continue to manufacture the TV140, which had been designed and developed in Winnipeg with the assistance of the federal loan.[14] Without the TV140, the plant would be left with the four-wheel-drive tractors, the Cadillacs of the tractor world. They were a dangerously high-end product for farmers strapped for cash.

The union was not only determined to get out the message that the plant was important to the Manitoba economy, but also wanted to make it clear that the workers were not interested in buying their jobs. They had a collective agreement that was due to expire in the fall of 2000, and there were suggestions that the union reopen the contract to make concessions to attract a purchaser. As Rausch and McLaren put it in a letter to the Local 2224 membership, "Since 1978 Versatile has been placed in a sale position four times and each time the threat and blackmail of future job security has accompanied the sale. As recently as late 1998/early 1999 the Company attempted to get the Union's agreement for concession by entering early bargaining." In each of those cases the union had withstood the pressure to open the contract and make concessions—and in each subsequent round of bargaining it had won contract improvements.

The union also had two other serious problems on its agenda. Even if the Versatile plant had not been faced with a forced sale or a shutdown, most of its members were in dire financial straits. In July 1998 Versatile had laid off four hundred workers. Even the workers who were not laid off were essentially working half-time because the company was on a four-weeks-on, four-weeks-off schedule. "The way the layoffs have been structured it's been difficult for our senior members to find work," Rausch said. "Most of our members are over forty-five and need help with retraining, resumes, counselling, and the proper procedure to find work."

Despite the union's numerous requests, the company refused to set up a worker adjustment committee to help workers with expired EI claims move into other careers. In a news release Rausch argued that the company could afford an adjustment program: "Versatile has a program set up for its laid-off salaried staff. In the past three years New Holland has acquired over a dozen corporations worldwide worth billions of dollars."[15] It was almost impossible for the workers on the one-month-on, one-month-off cycle to find work during the months they were off work, because, as McLaren and Rausch together pointed out, "No one will hire you for a four-week period knowing you will return to your job at the end of it."[16] The union also approached the company in an attempt to spark interest in a program that would provide older workers with an incentive to retire, and also began seeking severance pay and benefits for workers who had little expectation of recall. The company rejected the request for a worker adjustment committee in a one-line letter.[17]

The other issue for the CAW was the company pension plan, which was underfunded by nearly $11 million. Although the CAW had negotiated a number of significant increases in the Versatile pension plan, the plan would not have to pay them out for several years until a larger percentage of the workforce retired. This time delay allowed New Holland to amortize its pension obligations over fifteen years, which in turn created the $11-million unfounded liability. Under normal circumstances this liability would not have been a problem, but if New Holland, or another subsequent owner, decided to wind down the pension plan, the company would have been under no legal obligation to fund the difference between the amount then in the plan and the amount owing. Paterson and the CAW's Chernecki recognized that if New Holland did not find a buyer, it might simply close the plant and walk away from an $11-million obligation. Paterson met with NDP Labour Minister Becky Barrett, who recognized that this was not just an issue for the Versatile workers but a potential problem for all workers with pension plans. In March 2000 the NDP government amended pension regulations, requiring employers who shut down pension plans to fund any shortfall in direct benefit pension plans within five years of the date of termination of the plan. This new regulation was similar to regulations existing at that time in Alberta and Ontario.

During the talks that the CAW and the government conducted in 2000 Paterson also suggested to Doer that the Manitoba government consider taking an equity position in Versatile to ensure that the jobs and technology remained in Manitoba. The proposal was not publicly pursued at that point, but the CAW would come back to the idea of public ownership in the following year.

Meanwhile, New Holland had been able to attract only a handful of potential bidders for Versatile. While federal, provincial, civic, and union officials were itching to fly down to Chicago to speak with Caterpillar executives, Caterpillar was expressing no interest in buying the firm. A variety of firms were rumoured to be interested in the plant, but only four showed up to take a look: Buhler, AGCO, the Winnipeg-based implement manufacturer MacDon, and a New Holland dealer from Texas. CAW onlookers were of the opinion that the company's unco-operative attitude had frustrated potential buyers. In the end only Buhler was prepared to make a bid.

The provincial government officials involved saw Buhler as a made-in-Manitoba solution. Besides, you could not argue with success, and Buhler had enjoyed plenty of that. In his discussions with the province, Buhler indicated that he would be looking for changes in the CAW contract. For their part, the union leaders decided not to contact Buhler, let alone support his bid, because they believed doing so would only put them on the road to concessions.

The federal government had serious reservations about Buhler. Federal officials doubted that he had the financial resources to compete in the international tractor market, and they were alarmed by his lack of a business plan. Not having a business plan was, of course, simply a part of the "Buhler logic." Moreover, the federal government had concerns about Buhler's ability to take on the $32-million loan. When this issue arose, the provincial government lobbied Ottawa, essentially on Buhler's behalf, in an attempt to ensure that the sale went ahead. As a result Buhler found himself negotiating from a position of strength despite the many reservations about his viability as a purchaser.

In early 2000 Versatile workers got another reminder that they were trapped between the devil and the deep blue sea. While they were unhappy that New Holland was being forced to sell the plant, a news story out of Antwerp was a grim reminder that Case New Holland was intent on reducing its global workforce. In February 2000 Case New Holland announced a planned elimination of seven thousand jobs over the next two years; it would close down ten plants and fifteen ware-houses.[18]

Buhler's bid for the Versatile operation had to be approved by the U.S. Department of Justice, which shared many of the Canadian government's reservations. The Justice Department had originally ordered New Holland to divest itself of the Versatile lines because it wanted to maintain a measure of competition in the North American tractor market. For that to happen Versatile would have to remain a viable, continent-wide operation. But Buhler lacked the capital to invest in large-scale production, and his dealer network was small—the dealers who sold Buhler products were, for the most part, not tractor dealers. If, as the Justice Department feared, a Buhler-owned Versatile failed, Case New Holland and John Deere would be left to divide the tractor market between themselves. As a result the Department was reluctant to approve the sale. An outraged Engel stated that he was astonished that "the U.S. Department of Justice can control the destiny of a Canadian-run, Canadian-born company." He was rather conveniently ignoring how if it were not for the Justice Department's initial ruling and its refusal to let John Deere buy the company, Buhler would never have had a chance of purchasing Versatile.[19]

Both Premier Doer and Manitoba Industry, Trade and Mines Minister MaryAnn Mihychuk wrote to federal Liberal Industry Minister John Manley urging the federal government to do all it could to facilitate the sale of the plant to Buhler. By that point the federal government had overcome its reservations about Buhler and joined him in lobbying the U.S. government. Industry Canada official Tony Jarvis told the news media that the Canadian government believed the Buhler bid was the best one possible. Federal External Affairs Minister Lloyd Axworthy met with U.S. Secretary of State Madeleine Albright to see if she would be prepared to put pressure on the Justice Department.[20] The arm-twisting worked, and the Department of Justice withdrew its objections. The final piece of the puzzle was the transfer of the $32-million loan from New Holland to Buhler.

Interestingly, prior to 2000 Buhler had for the most part refrained from making donations to political parties. However, in that year eight Buhler companies made donations to the Liberal Party for a total of $12,633. Most of the donations were for $1,250, but Buhler Industries gave $2,537 and John Buhler Inc. gave $2,006. Paterson always found

Buhler's sudden embrace of the Liberal Party and the Chrétien government's decision to champion Buhler's case in Ottawa to be, at best, highly coincidental.

Buhler wanted the loan but was not interested in providing a loan guarantee. New Holland could have continued to guarantee the loan except that the Department of Justice ruling had stipulated that New Holland could not provide financing to whichever company ended up purchasing Versatile. If New Holland was not divested from the loan by the end of June 2000, it was expected that the Justice Department would oversee the sale of Versatile. In the Canadian government's view this would have resulted in the closing of the plant and the transferring of the product lines to the United States. Thus, in what was to turn out to be one of the most controversial elements of the deal, the government transferred the loan to Buhler without securing a guarantee of repayment. In its rationale for this decision the government stated:

> Co-operation in maintaining the operation will demonstrate the Canadian government's continued support for the agricultural portions of the economy, especially at a time when farm receipts in the West are at a low point in their business cycle. It will maintain 350 existing direct jobs and the research and development, the capital investment and local spinoff benefits will continue. Canadian farmers will continue to have a choice to purchase Canadian-made tractors.[21]

New Holland had begun repaying the loan in 1997, but Buhler was given a holiday on loan payments. Under the amended agreement he would pay the federal government the money owing to it over a ten-year period starting in 2003. The government's analysis of the loan transfer acknowledged that the loss of the "loan guarantee may raise the risk of default," but still it concluded, "Industry Canada is satisfied with Buhler Versatile's business plan to conduct its operations and pay back the loan."[22] The reference to the business plan is ironic given the federal government's earlier anxieties about the lack of same. It was Industry Canada's position that with no one else interested in the plant, it had little choice but to give the deal to Buhler. Industry Canada representative John Mihalus said, "It could have been a deal breaker. That would probably have meant the plant would be closed and the jobs would have gone to the U.S. Keeping the jobs in Winnipeg was the key for us." The details of the loan guarantee received no publicity at the time. All the obstacles had been removed for Buhler's rescue of the plant.

As the agreement was being hammered together McLaren got several phone calls from someone who claimed to have inside information on the deal. The person told him about being at certain meetings and made it clear that the union was "getting screwed over in this deal." The implication in the calls was that New Holland was giving the plant to Buhler in the expectation that he would shut the plant down. McLaren told the caller "that we had our suspicions but we needed some evidence." The mystery caller was not able to provide any documentation that backed up the allegations. While the calls did not provide the union with anything tangible, they heightened McLaren's suspicions of Buhler and his intentions.

In mid-June Buhler announced that Buhler Versatile Inc., a wholly owned subsidiary of Buhler Industries Inc., would be taking over the Versatile plant from New Holland. To run the plant Buhler would go on to create Buhler Versatile Industries (BVI) as a wholly owned subsidiary of Buhler Industries Inc. As part of the deal, Buhler would be getting the rights to the Versatile four-wheel-drive tractor and the Genesis tractor, which would be relaunched by Buhler's distribution system as the Buhler Versatile and Buhler Genesis tractors in January 2001. The company's new release continued:

> In addition, Buhler will supply New Holland North American dealers with the 2WD Genesis and 4WD Versatile tractors until October 31, 2001 and New Holland dealers outside of North America until December 31, 2002. Buhler will also supply the Winnipeg produced replacement parts for the tractor lines on an ongoing basis and will continue to manufacture the TV140 Bi-Directional tractor exclusively for New Holland distribution.[23]

In an article that appeared on the Buhler Web page, Engel argued that under Buhler's ownership Versatile would provide Canadian farmers with "a non-major that competes aggressively in the marketplace on price." Unlike the major tractor manufacturers, he said Buhler would run a lean, cost-conscious operation, joking, "We don't have 27 vice-presidents flying around the world first-class." Engel argued that buying the firm at a low point in the farm economy's cycle made sense because it would allow the company to be ready to take advantage of the expected economic rebound. Engel said he had been overwhelmed by calls from dealers interested in carrying the Versatile tractors. "There's an awful lot of good dealers out there who are sick and tired of dealing with the majors."[24]

There was no information provided at the time as to how much Buhler had paid for the company, although various news reports put the figure at near $100 million. If that were indeed the price, he would have had to pay $68 million in cash and assumed liability for the $32-million loan.[25] While Buhler assumed liability for the federal loan, New Holland also agreed to top up the $11-million shortfall in the Versatile pension plan and provide a severance package for the salaried employees. Buhler had also asked for a severance package for the unionized workers, but New Holland turned him down. As Michael Decter comments:

> What could go wrong? Mr. Buhler could get carried away with his own success and make a bad acquisition in the field; his skills may not prove successful against the declining market. To date, he has avoided this problem; his approach has been to pay the lowest possible price for all new assets, which is an important factor in his success.[26]

The $100-million figure would prove a bit of an exaggeration. Buhler came by his reputation as a bottom-feeder honestly. As time would reveal, Buhler had certainly paid the lowest possible price for the Versatile operation.

6

Negotiations

Summer to Fall 2000

As members of the Local 2224 bargaining committee began to prepare to negotiate their first contract with John Buhler, they knew an economic storm was blowing through the farm-implement industry. North American tractor sales remained stagnant: in 2000 only 448 four-wheel-drive tractors were sold in Canada. The market for two-wheel-drives was stronger, but still depressed: in 2000 Canadian dealers sold 2,979 of them.[1]

Even before Buhler had bought the plant, he had been sending out messages to the provincial government that he would be looking for concessions. In response the bargaining committee attempted to negotiate a new contract before the sale went through, writing to Versatile human resources vice-president David Morgan on July 6, 2000, proposing that talks start as soon as possible.[2] As Dale Paterson put it, an agreement with New Holland would provide the new owner with labour stability until a new relationship could be established. The company, not surprisingly, was not interested.

Premier Gary Doer was also worried about what might happen in negotiations. During the time when he worked to gain federal government approval for the loan to Buhler he had come to realize that the Versatile negotiations could be disastrous. The union had made it known that it would prefer to see just about anyone other than Buhler owning the plant. Buhler said that while he could work with a union, he would prefer to work with a union other than the CAW. Later, looking back on events, Doer remembered meeting with his senior advisor (and former Pawley government cabinet minister) Eugene Kostyra and saying, "The owner wants a different union, the union wants a different owner, we are headed for trouble." As a result the government took the unusual step of offering pre-bargaining mediation: an offer that both parties rejected.

For its part, the CAW found itself no longer dealing with a multinational corporation with an international network of dealers and hundreds of millions of dollars of resources. The members may not have liked Buhler, but they knew that if they were going to keep their jobs the plant would have to continue to be competitive and profitable. Given the CAW's grave doubts about Buhler's ability to run the plant over the long run, an argument could be made for taking a concessionary approach to bargaining. But the concerns for the long run had to be tempered with financial information being leaked to the union that indicated Buhler had struck a sweetheart deal with New Holland. According to this information, Buhler had not had to put up any cash for the plant—instead New Holland had given him the plant, paid him to assume the loan, and was buying tractors from Buhler on a cost-plus basis: an incredible deal. If the information was correct—and it seemed that it was—the union calculated that Buhler would want to keep workers in the plant, making tractors. Why, the bargaining team wondered, should they make concessions to a man who had just had a company handed to him on a silver platter?

Paterson recalled suggesting that the Local focus on "getting a collective agreement that may not be the world's greatest, but would give us some stability." He reminded the bargaining committee that the status quo might be better than the alternative. The union "had huge debates" about the direction it should take in bargaining; the bargaining team, with members from each department in the plant, was coming under pressure to take an aggressive position. Patterson suggested that by making concessions they could go on to get a sense of what Buhler could do with the plant. "I pointed out that he has a record of success, I don't care what you say, he's a successful businessman. How he does it is questionable but he is successful, he didn't get his money by being stupid." But for the most part the Local was not interested in soft-pedalling its proposals. According to Paul Lussier, most of the Local members favoured treating the negotiations as simply another round in which the union would "do what it had always done, win some increase in benefits and improvements in pension."

The developing of the bargaining position was played out against the highly competitive background of politics in Local 2224. Len Rausch and Peter Magda had led Local 2224 through the 1980s, with Rausch serving as the plant chair and Magda as Local president. In 1988 Cliff Anderson, another veteran of the early organizing drive, defeated Magda as president. When Anderson resigned before completing his term of office, he was replaced by vice-president Stan Letwyn. The 1994 elections saw Magda win election as Local president, with Felix Adolphe elected plant chairperson. The result was viewed as a victory of the left caucus in the plant, although Adolphe, as a former leader of the Hydraulic Engineering Workers Association, was not a left-winger.

Len Rausch and Scott McLaren were initially dismayed and angered by the outcome of the 1994 election in which Rausch lost his position as plant chairperson, and McLaren had lost his position on the plant committee. Rausch concluded that every politician has a sell-by date and he had, at least temporarily, reached his. After nine years of intense union activism he was grateful to have some time to himself again. In the following years he built himself a new home at Matlock, just north of Winnipeg on Lake Winnipeg. Looking back on the election, McLaren said, "In a sense people thought it was time for a change. A lot of us had been around for a long time and I understand that. I had considered staying out of union politics. I thought, 'I've done my share. I get to go home at night, I actually have a life, I can do things on the weekend.'" Still, neither of them was able to completely turn his back on the union. McLaren became active in the health and safety committee, and Rausch remained involved in the life of the Local in general. In 1997 both of them were returned to office, Rausch as president, McLaren as plant chairperson.

In that position McLaren was to play a key leadership role during the strike. Although he was an NDP supporter, he had emerged as a figure who could bridge many of the divisions in the plant. According to Lussier, who had been one of Magda's supporters, McLaren was seen as a neutral figure. "Both sides tried to court Scotty. He's a smart man, he's got a mind of his own, and he'll do what's right for the membership." Louis Mora said that he and many members would "trust Scott with their lives; trust what he thought, trust what he said."

The first sign that life at Versatile was going to change dramatically came in the way that the company treated its non-union employees: secretarial staff, accounting, engineers, foremen. To allow them to qualify for severance pay, New Holland had fired all 135 of its non-union employees. Buhler rehired most of them but placed them on six month's probation, with reduced benefits. One of the people who was not rehired was the vice-president of human resources, David Morgan.[3] Lussier was disturbed by these developments.

> There were all these management people I worked with for years.
> I had good relationships with some of them and bad relationships

with some of them. But I mean I truly felt for these people in management.... I thought, "If John Buhler's treating these people like this, what's it going to be like when we go into negotiations?"

These anxieties were exacerbated at Buhler's first meeting with the employees. According to Lussier:

> He just waltzed into the plant like he had taken over the world. We're all assembled in one of the paint shops and he's standing up and saying how he's going to do this and this and how he was the only guy that wanted to buy it and he's got big plans for this plant. But you look around and you see the plant manager sitting off to the side on a pallet with his head down. He's holding his head in his hands looking like he's about to cry. Well, if you can't convince your top guy [about] what you're saying, how are you going to convince the people on the floor?

When Buhler put the salaried staff on probation, many of the senior engineers began to look for other work. Ed Balik recalled that a good number of the engineers left as soon as they could. "They said they would not work for him. You know they have better connections than those of us who worked on the floor—they are friends with engineers all over." Versatile had been an industry leader; now, without an advanced engineering department, it seemed the company's days were numbered. After all, engineers did everything from glass to cabs, from hydraulics to electrical and electronics, from rubber to transmissions, axles, and gears. Rausch commented, "We had some of the best, you know, we had some of the best." Buhler's steps in this regard inspired both fear and anger. Employees concluded that, as an outsider, Buhler was jeopardizing their company.

As a result the bargaining team, despite Paterson's cautions, was not prepared to cut Buhler much slack. Lussier pointed out:

> This local has always challenged Dale. I mean, he's always the straight, calm guy in things like this. But he kind of thought, "You know what, maybe it might be best if we give the guy the opportunity to try and run this." But in the end Dale always listens to the bargaining committee.... Dale might think you're wrong, but Dale's there to guide us, he's not there to force us to do something. You ultimately make the decision and you live with it. And Dale makes that very clear to you.

The initial bargaining proposals included a number of provisions that the CAW fully expected to have to give up during the course of negotiations. The key issues, given the age of the workforce, were pensions and seniority. As McLaren explained, "Our focus at that point was not on wages, it was on maintaining our benefits, it was about getting better pensions and benefits."

McLaren believed it was important, before the union finalized its initial proposals, to get one particularly contentious question settled. He and the rest of the plant committee enjoyed super seniority when several hundred members were on layoff, and this was becoming a point of contention. Those who opposed super seniority argued that it amounted to a form of discrimination, while those supported the provision said it provided for continuity and protected union leaders from company harassment. Understandably, Local members who were on layoff, including former Local president Magda, were among the harshest critics of the provision. While the debate was at times acrimonious, in the end the membership voted to continue to support the inclusion of a super seniority clause in the contract.

In its opening position the CAW proposed a ban on contracting out, an increase in the size of the bargaining unit, two extra days of holiday, a full discussion of the layoff and recall procedures and salary (there was no specific wage proposal), and improvements in the pension and benefits plan, including a provision that would encourage workers to take early retirement. It was a fairly rich package, and the bargaining team did not expect to win it all. At the same time no one was prepared to listen to Buhler plead poverty. Days before negotiations started, the *Winnipeg Free Press* reported that Buhler's business operations had reported a record $100 million in sales. The story predicted that the company could double over the next year thanks to the Versatile acquisition.[4]

Bargaining opened on September 29, 2000, at the CAW offices, with Buhler, entirely on his own, telling the assembled union reps "You're not getting a dime" and presenting the union with a point-form proposal that he assured them they were not going to like. If Buhler believed that by leaving wage rates alone he would be able to force through the changes he was looking for, that position was a misreading of the union's concerns over seniority and benefits. The bargaining committee was quickly angered by Buhler's condescension, his lack of preparation, and even his confusion about what existed in the current collective agreement. It was such a strange performance that they remained uncertain about the owner's intentions. McLaren eventually concluded that either Buhler simply thought the union would accept his proposals or he hoped to goad it into a strike. In either case, when Buhler returned to the plant after that first meeting, he told employees that he expected the union to accept his proposals.

To counteract this message, the bargaining team made four hundred copies of Buhler's proposal and distributed them to the membership. From that moment onwards the momentum for a strike began to build quickly. According to McLaren, the members wanted to know why the union was not going out on strike immediately. "Our biggest problem at that time was going back to the membership and saying to them, 'No, guys, we're not going on strike tomorrow, we're going to negotiate this contract.' After seeing that first offer our guys were telling us, 'What are you waiting for?'" Bargaining team member Winston Johnson had the same recollection: "The membership instruction was, 'Listen, you guys are wasting time, let's set a deadline. Quit talking and let's walk.' They were very adamant about that."

Whether it was in the bar, in committee meetings, or in his office, Paterson kept trying to hold the bargaining team back. "At one point I was suggesting, why not just keep working after the contract expired? Why force the issue? Why not let him see if he can run the company? But Buhler kept egging them on. They'd had enough of him, with his 'I've got a lot of money, you're not going to get any of it.'" Because the bargaining team members all knew that labour costs represented only a very small portion of the cost of a tractor, they did not believe there was a strong argument for big cuts in their benefits. The union members might have agreed to a wage freeze in the hopes of winning increases when the economy improved, but they also knew that the proposed cuts to benefits and seniority would not be easily reversed.

At the second bargaining session, held on October 18, Buhler had nothing more in writing to present to the union. Instead he told the committee that letters of agreement dealing with severance pay, job protection due to outsourcing, early retirement provisions, and a wage security plan "wouldn't survive." He also said that he intended to "get rid of seniority" so that he could transfer employees as he saw fit. Buhler told the bargaining team that AGCO had recently contacted him to see if he was interested in selling the plant to them. Aware of the union's fears that AGCO would buy the company only to shut it down, during negotiations Buhler regularly raised the possibility of a sale to that company.

For the most part Buhler simply reiterated his previous position. He did not provide any details on the Buhler benefit package, nor did he provide specifics about his concerns over seniority. Paterson asked if

Buhler would come to the table with a manager who knew the plant, hoping that through discussions it might be possible to find some solutions to any problems that were hurting productivity. By the end of the meeting Buhler was making it clear that the only way he believed he could keep the plant alive was to bring wages down to $13 or $14 an hour. Bargaining team member Winston Johnson concluded that Buhler's overall goal was to reduce wages and salaries to the level at his other operations. "He said he can't pay us more than he pays other guys." In other words, when the plant was transferred from New Holland to Buhler, the workers were transferred from the world of the core labour market to the peripheral labour market.

During this same session Buhler said that he wanted people working from buzzer to buzzer, adding that he had recently come across a plant worker reading the newspaper. The worker had also not given him what he considered a proper greeting. McLaren later made some inquiries and spoke to the worker, who explained that it had happened on his lunch break and that on his own time he did not have to talk to anyone he did not want to speak with—and that was certainly how he felt about Buhler.

On the following day Buhler came accompanied by plant manager Ken Kidd and human resources officer Helen Bergen. Bergen outlined the benefit package, which covered a wide range of services up to a value of $1,000 a year; employees also had the ability to carry over that portion of the benefit that they had not used up. The CAW team quickly realized that their current benefit plan was far superior to the one that Buhler was offering them. In fact, the Manitoba Labour Board would later conclude that the CAW plan was worth $700,000 per year more than the Buhler plan.

Kidd explained that in order to get specific jobs done the company wanted the right to transfer workers from one department or job to another without regard to seniority. Paterson pointed out that the company already had that right in a number of cases. When Lussier backed up Paterson's point by explaining that as an assembly worker he would be forced to take a temporary transfer whether he wanted to or not, regardless of seniority, Buhler said, "No, you can quit if you don't want the job." In an effort to clarify what was being requested, McLaren said, "You want to be able to pick and choose the people *you* think can do the job." Buhler said, "That's management's job to pick the people. I know you don't like the way I think. I didn't build my empire on having people not work." Looking at the union's notes and reflecting on this exchange after the strike, Paterson ruefully commented that this was a perfect example of the difficulty of bargaining with Buhler. First of all, the company had yet to put detailed language on the table; therefore the union was never clear about what Buhler was proposing. Secondly, while Kidd had at least addressed a specific element of the agreement, Buhler tended to speak in confrontational generalities. The exchange left union members uncertain as to what was being proposed and doubtful that Buhler understood the contract.

As he listened to Buhler speak about seniority in this dismissive fashion, Lussier found himself thinking about the men at the plant who were fifty or sixty or sixty-three years of age. "Where would these guys be under him? They wouldn't be working there, because seniority would mean nothing." It was difficult enough working in a heavy industrial setting for twenty or thirty years—"Sooner or later your body's going to give out. I mean, I'm a young big man, that place just blew my shoulders out from working there. You know you're always holding a thirty-pound impact gun or something like that. It takes its toll on the body." Fellow bargaining team member Mel Resler was thinking similar thoughts: "Just because you're older and you can't work as fast as you were when you were younger, you know, that shouldn't make a difference. You're one of the guys that helped build that company up into what it was before it was sold. And I realized that even though I had twenty-seven years' seniority, that time didn't mean anything to him."

As the meeting broke up, Buhler said, "I hope you consider my proposals because I am all you've got. I have the upper hand on the union because nobody will like the outcome. I'm asking you to look at it, but for now I have the upper hand.... AGCO wants the problem. Maybe I should tell them, have it, but they don't want to keep it here."

Resler was shocked by the initial proposals. He viewed them as unrealistic, but like most members of the bargaining team he thought that Buhler would back off of the proposals over time. "But he moved in the other direction the next time. I thought we would try to get to the happy medium, but his happy medium was always going down." Like other members of the bargaining team, Resler concluded, "There's no way this man's going to move unless we do go out on strike."

At times a strike vote is simply just a tactical manoeuvre, a way for the members to signal to management their support for the bargaining team. No union is obliged to go out on strike merely because the members have provided it with a strike mandate. The Versatile employees were no strangers to either strikes or lockouts. They had gone through a five-week lockout in 1985 and a nine-day strike in 1994. But a strike this time would be very different from anything the members had ever experienced. Strikes are usually measured in days and weeks, rather than months. This time McLaren was warning members, "This is a guy who is going to make you stand out there for six months." No matter how often he put this message out, the members still seemed to believe that Buhler would give up within two or three weeks.

As long as Buhler was determined to gut the benefit plan and the seniority system, the only response, it seemed, was to go on strike. Buhler appeared to be determined to get rid of the older workers. When Bill Sokoliuk heard about Buhler's plans for seniority, he began to think about his thirty-six years in the plant and he figured, "Holy God, I'm the first guy out of the door if he gets what he wants." Not surprisingly, he supported the union. "I worked too long for all those years to lose that all." James Mateychuk had the same thoughts. "We would not have been getting those benefits if we did not have a union. Everything was good—pension was good, dental was good, you didn't have to pay for your prescription drugs. If you give up your seniority, you might as well leave." Ray Wilkie, who had been with Versatile since 1975, also pushed for a strike vote. "What was the big issue? The seniority. That was the big issue, because if he got rid of seniority, all the guys know we'd be gone."

Buhler may have been the CAW's worst nightmare come true, but in the United States the newly merged Case New Holland was also taking an aggressive approach in its negotiations. The company made it clear to the UAW that its overall plan was to reduce its global workforce by 7,200. UAW president Stephen P. Yokich called CNH's consolidation plan "another example of a multinational corporation with multi-billion-dollar revenues throwing highly-skilled, experienced and productive workers overboard in the wake of a merger."[5] In the summer of 2000 the company announced that if the union did not give way on seniority provisions in the existing contract it would close its two-wheel-drive tractor plant in Racine, Wisconsin, where the J.I. Case Company had been founded in 1844. According to the UAW, Case was threatening to shift the jobs and production to its plant in Fargo, North Dakota.[6] After the state government agreed to come up with $5.63 million in incentives and the UAW made some last-minute concessions, Case agreed to keep the jobs in Racine. The agreement called for converting the Case tractor manufacturing operations to assembly-only for two-wheel-drive tractors. New Holland tractors, along with those carrying the Case name, would be assembled at the Racine plant.[7]

In Winnipeg, following the October 19 bargaining session, the bargaining team resolved to ask the membership for a strike mandate. Johnson recalled that Paterson was still urging caution. "Whatever the membership wants Dale will support, 'no ifs, ands, or buts.' But he always encouraged us to make sure that this was what our membership wanted." According to Johnson, Paterson would go to each bargaining committee member and ask, "What is your membership's position on this?" Paterson warned the members that people who go out on strike always "have second thoughts."

At an October 22 meeting of the membership in the Dakota Hotel, the bargaining team outlined Buhler's proposals, the steps the union had taken to move negotiations forward, and their frustrations. They hoped that a strike vote might convince Buhler that the benefits and seniority were important to the members and not just to the bargaining committee. McLaren, Rausch, and Paterson also made it clear that Buhler had sent out signals that any strike would be a long one. McLaren was blunt: "I said this is not going to be short-lived. This guy has lots of money, he can cannibalize this business if he wants." They would be in for the long haul.

This was not a case of the leadership cranking the members up to take strike action. One of the members pointed out that his wife's insulin bills came to $4,000 a year. Another member, angered by Buhler's attitude in the talks, said they had to show Buhler that "We are not a social club, we are a union." McLaren recalled warning members not to take on any new debt. He also promised that the bargaining team would bring any new proposals to the membership. Lussier remembered there being "very little problem in selling the members on a strike vote" after they had outlined Buhler's intentions regarding the health benefits and the seniority. "At this point the people working in the plant have been there for twenty years or more. These are all guys that have lived and died by this seniority clause." Not surprisingly, the vote in favour of strike action that night was overwhelming—197 in favour, 7 against.

Despite the warnings, many of the members remained unconvinced that the strike would be lengthy. Joseph Smith figured that it would last three or four weeks at the most. Johnson said he thought the strike would last a month. "After Buhler started losing money I thought he would buckle, call us back to the table and talk. As a worst-case scenario I thought he would have offered us what we were making at the time. I thought his proposal of cutting the collective agreement was a gimmick." Wilkie recalled asking McLaren how long he figured the strike would last. He was shocked to hear him predict it might last for six months. "But I didn't believe it. I didn't believe Scott."

When the union and Buhler met two days later, Buhler once again came to the session alone. He announced there was no hope for the factory. "Originally I wanted the contract the same as the Steelworkers [had in one of his other plants]." He said he was surprised by the members' decision to support strike action, claiming that the company was burdened with debt and could not afford a strike. For its part, the union had revised its proposals. Paterson also said the union wanted to speak with Kidd about the problems with seniority. He made it clear that the union needed some details as to the types of changes that the company was looking for. "If you have problems with job postings, talk to us."

In response Buhler spoke of his long-held dream of making tractors. According to McLaren he said, "God made me the custodian of a thousand employees. He told me this is my role in life." Lussier was taken aback by Buhler's reference to a mandate from a higher power. "I'm not saying that people don't have visions from God, I'm religious myself, I'm Catholic, but I've never had God tell me something like that."

Word of Buhler's reference to the Almighty quickly circulated through the Versatile plant. At the start of the next bargaining session, on Tuesday, October 31, Buhler, once more appearing at the table without any staff, apologized. He asked "Did I really say God spoke to me? God never spoke to me. What I meant is I have a God-given talent and that I have a vision of one thousand employees." Nevertheless, his language remained messianic at times. For instance, he often told the CAW team that when he had bought the plant it was essentially finished and that they ought to view him as their saviour—a phrase that rankled the union members who firmly believed that they had helped build the company.

By October 31 the union had divided its proposals into monetary and non-monetary matters, and it was prepared to talk about the non-monetary matters that day, the monetary ones two days later, and remain available for further discussions on the weekend.

As the talks continued that day, a controversy arose over the union's proposals for improved health and safety provisions (although it had dropped its proposal for a full-time health and safety officer). Buhler argued that with government health and safety regulations already in place there was no need for health and safety provisions in the contract, nor was he moved by McLaren's argument that the government regulations simply constituted the bare minimum for health and safety. When McLaren explained that the union wanted a computer disc containing the seniority list because he found himself spending too much time making requests for the list from management, Buhler said the request was essentially irrelevant because in the future McLaren would not be working for the union.

After several hours of discussion the two parties were only able to reach agreement on the names of a potential arbitrator, although Buhler made it clear he opposed grievances. He told the CAW team, "I hate grievances." One of the issues the union raised was the need to have more detailed information on job postings made available to the members. This, McLaren said, was necessary to ensure that all members had a fair chance to apply for vacant jobs. Buhler replied that while he wanted to be fair, he believed that seniority was not fair.

When Buhler once more stressed that he needed more flexible seniority rules to allow him to "bring back by department who I want," the bargaining team offered to go through the list of laid-off workers. By demonstrating to Buhler that most of the laid-off workers had extensive experience in many different departments in the plant, the team hoped to convince Buhler to drop his opposition to seniority. It was a disheartening exercise: as the bargaining team members went through the list, identifying the various departments that the laid-off workers had worked in over their careers, Buhler appeared to be unconvinced. Then, after simply hearing the man's name and without waiting to hear about his qualifications, Buhler announced that the eighth man on the list would be recalled. According to McLaren, "That made it clear to us that it was not about skill and ability, it was about his ability to pick and choose his favourites."

By that point in the talks the bargaining team members suspected that they were teaching Buhler about his own collective agreement. The union would raise an issue, such as health and safety, that had not been a part of Buhler's original package, and Paterson could see a light go on in Buhler's mind as the owner saw, apparently for the first time, an element of the agreement that was hitherto unknown to him. Now that he knew about it he wanted either to get rid of it or water it down. Paterson found himself becoming reluctant even to raise matters that needed to be resolved or improved.

Eventually Paterson told Buhler, "We are going backwards. I am trying to find a way for you and our committee to settle, but it's not going that way." Buhler responded that Paterson could do what he wanted, but if he thought a strike would get the members more, he should "just try me." Buhler then suggested that he was prepared to offer a status quo agreement. When Paterson asked Buhler what he meant by status quo, the owner said "What do you think I mean?" Paterson said, "Cover to cover?" Buhler said, cover to cover except for the letter of understanding that would prohibit the company from laying people off as a result of the outsourcing of work. For the union, that position was far less than status quo.

As the meeting was drawing to a close Paterson asked Buhler to look at the union's financial package, which had been reduced to a wage freeze in the first year, twenty-five cents an hour in the second and third years, and an improvement to the pension plan. The Manitoba Labour Board would later note that the union's new position "represented a significant reduction from its initial proposal." Buhler promised the union a written response in two days, by November 2, which was the day before the union's strike deadline.

In the following day or two, several of the plant supervisors approached Rausch and McLaren expressing their unhappiness with the new regime at Buhler. Since the CAW represented the technical, office, and professional staff at the large auto plants in Eastern Canada, Rausch and McLaren thought it would be worth a shot to attempt to organize the supervisors. Rausch said he tried "to convince them to stay out with us, because if everybody stayed out with us at that rate we'd probably be back there right now." In the end only one person signed up. According to Rausch, "These guys had been there for thirty years and they were fifty-two, fifty-three years old, maybe fifty-four, fifty-five, so he sort of had them over a barrel. Nobody's going to hire a fifty-four-year-old foreman, they just don't do that anymore."

The talks came to a head on November 2. Buhler arrived and told the bargaining committee what they already knew—namely that their benefit package was far richer than the one he was proposing. He suggested that the union go through its package and he would give verbal responses. As McLaren itemized the pared-down package, Buhler's answers alternated largely between "You can put a big 'no' next to that" to "Two-letter answer" to "The answer to that is 'no'," with the odd "I'll check into it" or "It's covered under my proposals." When the union came to the various letters of agreement at the end of the contract Buhler also expressed an unwillingness to live with them, even ones that he had not objected to previously. He wanted to get rid of both the supplementary unemployment benefit plan and the severance package. He wanted to amend much of the health and safety article, leaving for the most part only those provisions required by law.

A strike, it appeared, was unavoidable. Buhler warned the union that it was crossing the line. Indeed, in a stunning and contradictory example of "Buhler logic," he told the bargaining team that the plant would never open and that he would be out there in his blue jeans shipping tractors across the picket line.

7

The Strike Begins

November to December 2000

On Friday, November 3, Richard Ullmann was working in the machine shop when bargaining team member Mel Resler appeared in the department and quickly passed the word that it was time for all of the men to begin packing up for the walk out. The Versatile strike had started.

For Ullmann, with more than a decade of experience at Versatile, it was not the first time they had gone out on strike. "We felt that we would be coming back eventually." As things turned out, it would be the last day any of the CAW members would work at the company.

For many of them the day would long remain a painful memory. They had spent most of their adult lives inside those factory walls. Work at Versatile could be difficult, dirty, and at times dangerous, but the Versatile employees were proud of the firm, proud of the product, proud to be industrial workers. Years later Bill Sokoliuk had to wipe away tears as he spoke of leaving Versatile. "You know we were like a family there. I spent more time with some guys than I would with my wife. And we really got along good. Because I used to think, if I retire, man, I'm going to miss these guys."

John Buhler had antagonized his workers far more than he realized when he called himself their saviour and put down their union as a social club. The workers were looking to themselves for their own salvation. A strike is a contest that brings to the surface the underlying differences in the interests of workers and employers. It is a reminder that at its heart employment is a bargain through which an employer buys a worker's labour power, and that the employees' greatest weapon for improving the terms of that bargain is to collectively withdraw that labour.

Collective protests over wages and working conditions are as old as wage labour. Withdrawals of labour have been called strikes since 1768, when British sailors protested working conditions by lowering (or striking) the sails of their vessels, bringing all activity along the London docks to a halt. Early strikes were often viewed as mutinies or rebellions, and usually put down by force. The British Combination Acts of 1799 made unions and strikes illegal. In 1834 six British agricultural workers were exiled to the work camps of Australia for forming a union.

In colonial Canada immigrants who had fled famine in Ireland found themselves digging canals for starvation wages. When labourers on the Lachine and Beauharnois canals struck for better wages in 1843, the government called out the troops. The soldiers ended the strike by opening fire on the strikers, leaving five workers dead. When workers at the McCormick Reaper Workers in Chicago struck for the eight-hour day in 1886, a battle broke out between the strikers and strikebreakers. The police arrived and fired on the pickets, killing two strikers.

In Canada the labour laws slowly began changing only in the 1870s. The *Trade Union Act* of 1872 stated that unions were not illegal organizations. But even if union members could now no longer be jailed for simply joining a union or daring to go out on strike, union life was far from easy. There were no laws requiring employers to negotiate with a union, nor were there any laws that prohibited an employer from firing a worker who joined a union. There was also no prohibition on hiring replacement workers, commonly referred to as scabs, during a strike.

For a strike to succeed, workers had to do more than simply withdraw their labour. They had to campaign to make sure that no one else took their jobs or bought their employer's products while the strike was on. Thus was born the picket line, the human barricade that striking workers create around their workplace not just to keep replacement workers and supplies out but also to make members of the public aware of the strike. Picket lines, not surprisingly, have often been the scenes of violent conflict involving workers, strikebreakers, and security guards. In such situations the courts often intervene, issuing injunctions that place limits on the number of people who can picket at any one time and where they can picket. On occasion injunctions can even ban certain people from the picket line.

The first few days on the Buhler picket line were part festival, part demonstration, part riot. While the union eventually established a shift system, for the first week all the strikers were required to picket each day.

Ullmann recalled the first few days as "pretty jovial." The strikers hoped to put pressure on the company and get back to work. "We had lots of people out to show their solidarity." For Tom McCallum, the first days on the line were sheer chaos. "Everybody was wound up, I got wound up. It is easy to get your adrenaline up when your job is on the line and people are coming through the picket line. I don't know how to explain it—you are worried for your family so it really affects you." Ray Wilkie had been off on sick leave, but he asked his doctor to send him back to work. "I could have been off collecting benefits, but I wanted to be there and I wanted to support the union." One day a fuel truck driver refused to cross the picket line when he discovered that the plant was struck. As Ullmann recalled, "That was a good feeling—that other people would stand up with us."

When the strike started, plant manager Ken Kidd temporarily laid off all the non-union staff to reduce the potential for conflict. However, the company's decision to send several large trucks through the picket line in the early days of the strike prompted confrontation, particularly when one truck nearly ran down some strikers. As Stan Letwyn said, "When something like that happens you cannot control how people will respond. People broke off a mirror and were throwing stuff at the truck. They were pretty upset." By November 7 the company was complaining about the length of time it was taking to get vehicles through the picket line. While most vehicles were being held up for five to ten minutes, it took an hour and ten minutes and the support of the Winnipeg police to get one security guard through the line. The next day Buhler Versatile's Helen Bergen was complaining that the strikers were padlocking the gates and blocking the drive aisles, holding up a semi-tractor and trailer for an hour.[1]

In late November the Court of Queen's Bench granted a company request to prohibit the CAW from delaying vehicles entering the plant for more than three minutes and vehicles leaving the plant for more than five minutes. It did not, however, grant the company's request that the pickets be forced to wear identifying numbers and be forbidden to wear balaclavas. Instead it required both that picket captains be present at all times and that they provide the names of strikers who violated the injunction.

In most unions it is standard practice to have a strike preparation committee in each round of bargaining. Its responsibilities involve preparing for the strike that its members hope will not take place. As chair of Local 2224's strike action committee, John Pfeiffer, a twenty-five-year veteran at the plant, was responsible for ensuring that trailer, toilets, and furniture would be on site, and that picket signs, meals, and other supplies would be available from the start of the strike. As Pfeiffer recalled, the strikers showed tremendous skill and ingenuity. They built "what you could only call little houses" to set up outside the company gates. The houses were far more than lean-tos; they had walls, peaked roofs, and could hold about a dozen people. Because the CAW was renovating its Winnipeg offices, one of the houses even ended up with wall-to-wall carpets. One of the skilled electricians, John Rhoden, worked with Manitoba Hydro to run a power line to the site. With a chuckle Pfeiffer said, "We got an augur, dug holes, planted poles, and ran a power line. It was all metered, legal, and done to code."

A rented trailer just outside the main gate served as the strike headquarters. For the first few weeks Scott McLaren and Stan Letwyn virtually lived at the strike trailer, sleeping on folding cots. "Each morning," Letwyn said, "I woke up with terrible aches and pains." Bargaining committee member Paul Lussier kept McLaren informed of developments on the line, while Local president Len Rausch assisted members who were having problems with their financial institutions. Rausch also worked his large network of connections with non-union- ized employees and supervisors to develop an overview of what was going on inside the plant.

The plant had six separate gates, and an elaborate shift system had to be developed to ensure that each gate was covered at all times. Rob Rempel was in charge of putting together the weekly picket schedule. To qualify for the strike pay of $200 a week, the workers had to picket four to six hours, twice a week. That was the minimum; McLaren estimates that probably a hundred or so union members showed up every day of the strike to picket. The Local ran the picket line seven days a week, twenty-four hours a day: the only holidays during the strike were Christmas and Boxing Day. Because the union received donations from other union locals across the country it was on occasion able to supplement the $200 a week strike pay. Along with strike pay the union also paid the employer contribution on each member's contract benefit plan. Each picket received at least two sandwiches a day—one of Letwyn's main tasks was arranging meals, while Resler cooked smokies for the pickets. Other times Letwyn bought food from IGA and the nearby Texas Connection restaurant, which became a kind of unofficial strike headquarters. But the strike was still a tremendous hardship for workers used to making an average of $800 a week. Looking back on that period, Dwight Pitcher commented, "I went from $800 to $200—what are you going to give up, what do you ask your family to give up?"

One of the regular tasks was collecting wood for the fires that the strikers kept going in forty-five-gallon drums that the welders transformed into stoves. "We must have collected every piece of scrap wood in the city," McLaren said. "Our guys went to furniture stores, manufacturers, shippers—we picked up off-cuts, pallets, any wood that people did not need."

Picket captains like Wilkie and Ullmann were responsible for keeping track of who did and did not show up for their shifts and maintaining good relations with the police. They knew that an effective strike and buoyant morale depended on a strong and militant picket line. They also knew that too effective a picket line would draw a strong response from the police. Financial secretary Sandy Brar, who was proud of the union's militant record, said that he and the other strike leaders had to devote considerable energies to making sure that no one did anything hotheaded. At one point several tractors in the Versatile yard were vandalized, and although the culprits were never found, and may have been a group of teenagers, the union fell under suspicion. One of the strike committee's jobs was to make sure that the people most likely to cause dissension on the picket line always had work to do. As McLaren recalled: "We knew it could get very ugly. Our guys were mad. Some people thought I kept too tight a rein on things. But we were very conscious of how we looked in the media. We did do stuff that was wrong, we weren't perfect by any means, but we think we orchestrated a good campaign in the media." By the end, he said, "We weren't seen as the big bad union."

After the first week Kidd began recalling the salaried staff, putting them to work assembling tractors for a contract the firm had with Caterpillar. Although production was slow as office staff familiarized themselves with the equipment and the process, the plant was not completely shut down. Operations were further slowed down when Albert Lanoo, one of the supervisors, and Hugh Bagnall, the human resources manager, refused to cross the picket line. As a result they lost their jobs with the company.

Many of the union members had enjoyed relatively positive relations with Kidd, while others were angry because they thought he had facilitated the sale to Buhler and helped craft his bargaining plan. In the early weeks of the strike Kidd visited the strikers on the picket lines, bringing them coffee and, at times, even pizza. While some members viewed this simply as a continuation of their ongoing personal relations with Kidd, others viewed it as a sign of weakness. Because it was a potential source of division within the union, the strike leaders prohibited picketers from accepting food from management. Buhler and Engel also visited the picket line at various times, trying to put their case to the workers. Their overtures were usually rebuffed: most members believed that if Buhler wanted to end the strike he should be speaking to the bargaining committee, not to individual union members.

On one cold day Engel stopped to speak with the workers as he was leaving the plant, trying to convince them that they had not been getting the full story about what went on in bargaining. Off to one side McLaren, dressed in a snowmobile suit and balaclava, listened to the discussion for a few minutes and then stepped forward, removing his balaclava so Engel could see who he was. What, he asked, was the union not telling the workers? A crowd gathered as McLaren asked Engel if he had even attended any of the bargaining sessions. Engel acknowledged that he had not attended the sessions but had been informed about them by Buhler. He then attempted a joke to the effect that he might have just committed an unfair labour practice. McLaren told the people on the line that they had held Engel up for his allotted five minutes and they should let him pass.

The role of the police in a strike is often controversial. In a legal dispute between two private organizations—an employer and a union—the police are expected to remain neutral. However, employers often place demands on the police to enforce their private property rights—the right to deliver and ship goods, and the right to have staff, including strikebreakers, enter their properties.

Brar often found himself dealing with the police following confrontations on the picket line. For the most part, Brar said, the relations between the strikers and the police were positive, somewhat to his own surprise. Pfeiffer said that as long as the picketers were not, as he put it, overly rambunctious, the police did not interfere in their picketing. McLaren laughingly said, "There were a few times when they were rough," before adding that the police found it "hard to be brutal with a large group of people" when there were only two officers there. The police "would come out and tell you to stop doing something," Ullmann said, "but they were usually pretty good about things unless there had been some physical violence."

The one major complaint arose when the police informed McLaren that the company was bringing in a shipment of hazardous waste. Under no circumstances, the union was told, was anyone to try to stop this shipment. While McLaren believed that the waste was nothing more than a shipment of antifreeze, he contacted the local media and raised concerns about why Buhler was storing hazardous waste near a residential community. Despite the union's protests, the police provided the escort needed to get the shipment into the plant.

Relations with the company's security guards were far more contentious. The private security guards were equipped with video cameras and monitored the strikers for any violations of the court injunction. McLaren and Pfeiffer believed that the guards often tried to provoke problems on the picket line. At times McLaren and other union members suspected that they were being followed by security guards, and once Letwyn was confronted by security guards at a local shopping centre. McCallum said that the company's private security firm "was intimidating, and we were giving the same thing back. It is your family that is at stake. If you are not willing to fight for your family, well—throw in the towel." On occasion McLaren said police officers had to warn the security guards not to incite the pickets. During a long and bitter conflict there was only one arrest, the result of a shoving match between a striker and foreman.

From the start of the strike Buhler took the position in public that the plant could not be profitable without concessions from the union. "They know as well as I do that tractor sales were off by 50 per cent last year and another 50 per cent this year. I don't know what else I can do.... Farmers are already telling me the tractors are priced too high." In a reference to contracting work out, Buhler added, "If I bring work back into the plant, that will just increase costs."

Even if Buhler intended on undercutting the prices of other tractor manufacturers, the fact remained that labour constituted a very small percentage of the price of a Versatile tractor—which meant that cutting labour costs would not allow Buhler to give farmers a significant price break.

The union's major public relations challenge was to get people to realize that the strike had little to do with wages, but was a struggle over seniority, benefits, and job security. McLaren explained that the union saw the company proposals as an attempt to turn the factory into an assembly shop. He pointed out that even before Buhler appeared on the scene, "the machine shop had gone from 180 to 5, the sheet metal from 100 to 1 and the welders from 100 to 20."[2]

During the first few weeks of the strike the union and the company had little communication. On November 9 Buhler and CAW staff representative Dale Paterson spoke over the telephone, with Buhler indicating that he was not changing any of his positions. That same day Paterson heard rumours that Buhler was planning on bringing in a large number of strikebreakers. Alarmed by the prospect of violence on the line, Paterson arranged to meet Labour Minister Becky Barrett early the next morning at a Salisbury House restaurant on Ellice Avenue. Paterson said that if the employer brought in strikebreakers, the union would be forced to confront the government publicly with a demand for anti-scab legislation. To head off these possibilities, he proposed that the government appoint a mediator.

When Barrett eventually brought both sides together for a meeting in her office on November 22, Buhler indicated that he was interested in having the strike settled through arbitration—a process in which a third party, someone either agreeable to both the union and the company or appointed by government, dictates the terms of a new contract. Paterson argued that mediation would be more appropriate at that point. Mediation is similar to arbitration in that both parties make their case to a third party, who then attempts to find a way of bridging the differences. However, the mediator, unlike the arbitrator, does not have the power to impose an agreement. If mediation fails, the mediator prepares a report outlining the elements of what he or she believes would make an appropriate contract. While this report is not binding, it often forms the basis of a final agreement. For many very good reasons, unions and employers are both allergic to having agreements imposed upon them by people who do not have to live with the decision on a daily basis. Under mediation, both parties are more likely to move towards a compromise that they can live with rather than risk being criticized in the mediator's report if they fail to reach an agreement.

When Paterson suggested mediation, Buhler asked how much the process would cost. Paterson explained that the government, the union, and the employer would each pick up one-third of the cost. Buhler responded, "If it costs me, I'm not going." This position was to remain one of the most perplexing elements of the negotiations, because Buhler had just proposed arbitration as a solution, and he would have had to pay a third of the cost of that as well. It was also strange that Buhler, who seemed intent on imposing a radical rewrite of the collective agreement, wanted arbitration, because arbitrators are usually reluctant to impose major changes in a contract.

The provincial government's position was that the union should agree to arbitration. NDP Premier Gary Doer was concerned that the Versatile negotiations would not go well; arbitration was a chance, he thought, to salvage them. "We were recommending it to them. Our advice was take this, we are in the rapids here." The bargaining team concluded that arbitration was too extreme a measure to adopt at a relatively early point in the dispute. McLaren said:

We thought we should negotiate an agreement. In hindsight maybe we should have taken it. At that time we thought, "Let's get a mediator in here, maybe we can find some common ground, maybe Buhler will be more responsive, maybe we will be more responsive." We did not want arbitration because there are always problems with a contract that is imposed by someone else. Often they don't understand the important details, and these can cause problems for years to come.

With the company rejecting mediation and the union opposed to arbitration, the government appointed its director of conciliation and mediation services, Al Fleury, as a conciliator in the dispute. Unlike an arbitrator or a mediator, a conciliator is a government employee who can neither impose a settlement nor issue a public report. The conciliator is a sort of shuttle diplomat, someone who tries to bring the two sides closer together. Conciliators can play an important role when communications between the two parties have broken down, but they have little power to compel and cajole movement on either side of the table. The CAW's position at this point was that it had made a number of modifications to its initial proposal and was not likely to make any more until Buhler began to compromise. Instead the message that the union received from Fleury was that Buhler's position was getting worse, not better. Through Fleury, Paterson began to ask for a new written proposal from Buhler—the first and only one the union had received was the one-page sheet Buhler had presented on September 29 at the first bargaining session.

"I thought that maybe by the beginning of Christmas he would be willing to make a deal," Paterson said later. But as Christmas approached, Fleury told him that Buhler would not be able to provide a proposal until early in the new year.

A written proposal was important for another reason. McLaren and Rausch were starting to pressure Paterson to lay an unfair labour practice charge against Buhler. The information they had received from various sources had convinced them that New Holland had sold Buhler the factory for a song with the expectation that he would close it. McLaren believed that Buhler, as part of this strategy, "wanted to shut this place down and he wanted to be able to blame the union. We were getting the sense that he did not want an agreement." For Rausch and McLaren the pieces had started to fall together two or three weeks into the strike. "Len Rausch and I felt Buhler had bargained us into a situation where we had to strike. We thought we could get back at him by charging him with bargaining in bad faith." Under Manitoba labour law the union and the company have an obligation to attempt to reach an agreement—taking deliberate steps not to reach an agreement is considered bargaining in bad faith.

The *Manitoba Labour Relations Act* states, "It is in the public interest of the Province of Manitoba to further harmonious relations between employers and employees by encouraging the practice and procedure of collective bargaining between employers and unions." Given, then, that collective bargaining is in the public interest, the Manitoba government has passed laws encouraging the growth of such bargaining. Specifically, the rules require not only that employers and unions "bargain collectively in good faith with one another," but also that they "make every reasonable effort to conclude a collective agreement."[3] This approach is fundamentally different from the negotiations that take place between businesses and their suppliers, or between members of the public and retail vendors. In those negotiations the actors have no obligation to make every reasonable effort to reach an agreement. Indeed, most modern retail establishments simply post their prices on a take it or leave it basis. In collective bargaining, take it or leave it could well be taken as a sign of bargaining in bad faith.

Still, there is probably no more ambiguous concept in labour relations than that of bargaining in bad faith. The concept arises from a recognition that collective bargaining is both a test of the economic power of the employer and the union and the development of a continuing set of human relations. For this reason definitions of bad faith bargaining tend to focus not so much on the content of specific proposals but on how negotiations are carried out. Signs of bargaining in bad faith include comments made in the course of negotiations, inflexibility on central issues, or altering a position in the course of negotiations. Charges of bargaining in bad faith are heard by provincial labour board tribunals consisting of one labour and one employer representative and a government-appointed chairperson.

At that point in the strike Paterson was reluctant to take a bad faith charge to the Manitoba Labour Board. The CAW's preference is to settle its disputes on the picket lines and at the bargaining table, rather than through costly legal procedures at the Board. Paterson also questioned whether the union had the evidence needed to prove its case. The verbal communications between the conciliator, union, and employer, for example, cannot be submitted as evidence in a Labour Board hearing. Finally, on those rare occasions when labour boards do conclude that one party has bargained in bad faith, they often do little more than administer a slap on the wrists and tell both parties to go back to the table and bargain in good faith. In twenty years of collective bargaining Paterson had never laid an unfair labour charge: "Bargaining is about power, who's got the power. If you don't have the power, then please don't rely on the Labour Board to solve your problem for you." But McLaren and Rausch believed—correctly as it turned out—that this case was unique. As the strike dragged on, McLaren began to hound Paterson on a daily basis about laying charges. McLaren thought that the Local had all the evidence needed to make the case stick; indeed, he believed that Buhler would be the union's secret weapon. "We thought that if you put Buhler on the stand, he will tell you exactly what he did, we thought he would be our best witness. And in the end, he was."

On December 3, with winter setting in, the Local decided to invite family members for a day of picketing. Like many Versatile families Dwight and Cathy Pitcher were wondering whether they could afford the sorts of presents their two daughters had come to expect for Christmas. Suddenly the recently released movie version of Dr. Seuss's classic *How the Grinch Stole Christmas!* flashed through Cathy's mind. She grabbed a felt marker and a blank picket sign and dashed out a short message for her daughter Kailey to wear: "John Buhler, the Grinch who stole my Christmas." As she said later, "Everyone thought it was great." Except for John Buhler. That night when he drove up to the plant he saw the sign, stopped the car, got out and began to demand that the men take it down. Following a bitter exchange Buhler left, but the sign remained.

When the union complained about Buhler's behaviour, Bergen wrote a letter of apology on his behalf, promising that Buhler would not speak to the picketers again. The letter concluded with this explanation of Buhler's behaviour:

> You must understand that when Mr. Buhler saw the sign on the union trailer, he was truly disturbed. If you were one of the most generous men in Winnipeg, especially during the Christmas season, how would you react to such a sign? If you have any desire to continue the negotiations, I would suggest you remove the sign. In his heart Mr. Buhler was saving the jobs of the people when he purchased the Winnipeg factory and is deeply saddened by the reaction of the members.[4]

Buhler's mood was not improved when he read a lengthy satire that union members wrote based on *How the Grinch Stole Christmas!* This version ended not with the Grinch's redemption but with his death from a brain aneurysm.

In late December the union took its case against Buhler into Transcona, the home of his other Winnipeg plants, where Buhler had become involved in a local dispute over the future of a provincial government health office. When local residents became upset by a government decision to close a local health office, Buhler had offered to lease a True Value Hardware store location, which he had previously shut down, to the Winnipeg Regional Health Authority. He also said that over the next three to five years he was prepared to donate $500,000 to build a new health centre.[5] The CAW members questioned Buhler's commitment to health care, pointing out that he was in the process of trying to reduce their health benefits. They suggested that his generosity masked a desire to find a tenant who would pay for the renovation of his empty hardware store. According to Letywn, who helped lead this part of the union's anti-Buhler campaign, "Half a dozen of us from CAW went down to the community committee and handed out pamphlets and talked to residents one-on-one. We turned the tide." As a result of their efforts, no deal was made with Buhler.

As the first snows came, Sokoliuk thought, "We will never survive a winter. But we did. It's amazing. And at Christmas time, it was pretty touching." Letwyn found, "The atmosphere until Christmas was phenomenal on that line. I mean the solidarity, you wouldn't believe it." But if spirits were up, it was apparent that McLaren's predictions of a long strike were proving accurate. Some thirty non-unionized staff had been laid off. Fleury had been unable to get negotiations going again, and neither side was budging on seniority. No end was in sight.

8

The Threat of Plant Closure

January to February 2001

On January 15, 2001, the very nature of the strike changed when Buhler finally presented the union with a new written proposal, withdrew his November offer of binding arbitration, and announced that the firm would be hiring replacement workers.[1] Buhler official Craig Engel said the company would be using replacement workers and non-union staff to turn what he estimated to be $40-million worth of parts into tractors. In response Scott McLaren warned that strikebreakers would not be looked upon kindly by their co-workers once the strike ended—and that he did not have much confidence in their ability to build tractors. "They would be lucky to get two tractors a day out of there," the bargaining committee chairperson said.

At the same time as he was threatening to bring in strikebreakers, Engel also released the company's first-quarter financial statement, showing a 221 per cent increase in revenues. The increase was attributed to the sale of tractors stockpiled prior to the start of the strike.[2]

The new written offer also changed Dale Paterson's assessment of the union's ability to win a bargaining in bad faith charge. As he read through the proposal, the CAW staff representative Paterson thought, "Ah ha. Now we have him." It was the first time the union got a clear sense of just what it was that Buhler wanted. "During our negotiating sessions you could write down what he said to you, but it was like nailing Jell-O to the wall, he was always adding and changing things." Now Paterson could say, "He is bargaining backwards." The company had not only refused to compromise on any of its positions on benefits, seniority, or contracting out, but was also now proposing additional changes. For the first time Buhler was calling for the end of:

- provisions that gave workers with seniority preference when it came to shift assignments;

- provisions that ensured that all workers had a fair chance at overtime;
- two to three days of paid vacation between Christmas and New Year;
- the supplemental unemployment benefit that topped up workers' wages when they were laid off;
- severance pay—worth approximately $12 million; and
- health and safety training.

Other new proposals called for an increase in the number of hours a worker had to put in to qualify for full vacation with pay. The contract's definition of time worked was also to be amended to exclude workers on Workers' Compensation. The period of time that a laid-off worker would have a right of recall would be reduced from four years to two years. Buhler also called for further deletions to the health and safety article in the contract and super seniority was to be reduced. Finally, Buhler's plans for the future of seniority were clarified by his call, for the first time, of the deletion of Article 16.06, which stated:

> The Company and the Union agree with the principle that those with the greatest seniority shall be given preference in promotions and that those with least seniority shall be the first to be demoted or permanently re-assigned, providing that in either case, the employee or the employees involved, will have the opportunity to demonstrate skill and ability to effectively perform the job to be filled.

In the September 29 proposal, seniority had only been touched on in the company's proposal to "resolve ability to transfer employees," a proposal that would suggest some tweaking of the seniority provisions. In his comments at the table Buhler had indicated that he wanted to do away with seniority, but now he was putting forward a proposal in writing for the flat-out elimination of seniority in promotion and transfer. The company also wanted to delete the entire five-page layoff and recall article, which stated that layoffs were to be governed by a system of plant-wide seniority. The article was to be replaced with a "policy whereby layoffs will be by department according to seniority and classification." Many of the Versatile employees could remember the old days of departmental seniority in which employees that management wanted to keep were transferred into new departments shortly before layoffs were announced. The senior workers left in the department would then be vulnerable to layoffs if the layoffs were restricted to that department. Buhler also called for provisions that would not allow union members to represent people at grievance procedures on company time.

Moreover, these proposals were "dependent on negotiating a satisfactory 'return-to-work agreement.'" Return-to-work agreements, as the name suggests, are protocols that spell out the conditions under which employees are to be recalled to work. Not surprisingly, the CAW and Buhler would differ over the role of seniority in any return-to-work agreement.

By the time they received Buhler's new written offer, Paterson's copy of the labour code was well thumbed and festooned with yellow sticky notes. Paterson believed that even though Buhler had been elusive and ill-prepared, the union did not have the evidence needed to lay a charge of bargaining in bad faith. According to Paterson, based on everything the union had on the owner up to that point, the Labour Board, at the most, would have said, "You've been a bad boy, now go and bargain properly." But now the contents of the new proposal underscored the pattern that the union would have to establish to prove a charge of bargaining in bad faith. Paterson reasoned that if the union laid a strong, well-documented charge, demanding millions in back pay, the pressure would "bring Buhler to his senses and get him to finally negotiate an agreement."

McLaren felt vindicated. "Dale now thought we had at least enough to lay a charge. With this written offer we could clearly show that when we take stuff off, he's adding stuff on. We could show the first day's proposal and say, 'Here is his list of takeaways in September. Now look at his January 15 offer and see the things that have been added.'"

Paterson still needed the authorization of the CAW's national office in Toronto to lay an unfair labour practice charge—and that authorization was not forthcoming. The view from head office was still that these bargaining in bad faith charges were costly, hard to prove, and ineffective.

In public Craig Engel argued that the company had been forced to withdraw its offer of binding arbitration because it had just lost the contract to supply Case New Holland with the TV140 bidirectional tractor. He would later testify that on January 12 CNH informed him that because Buhler Versatile had failed to meet its obligation to supply the tractors, it was cancelling the contract with Buhler and moving production to its plant in Fargo. According to the agreement between Buhler and Case New Holland, Engel had the option of asking for ten days of grace to attempt to make good on the contract. Instead of exercising this option and going to the union in hopes of reaching an agreement, he chose to sell $10-million worth of TV140 parts inventory to CNH. Now Buhler was saying that the future of the plant had been riding on the contract, which he valued at $100 million. According to Engel, "The union was very much aware of that. The big future was with that tractor. It's a huge loss." Paterson's response was that Buhler had not informed the union about the pending loss of the TV140 contract.[3] There is no doubt that if the TV140 contract was truly lost, the plant's future was far less certain. The number of jobs would drop dramatically, as would the plant's profitability.

Buhler began to look for replacement workers—but to everyone's surprise his help-wanted ads appeared in newspapers in Fargo, North Dakota, rather than Winnipeg. The government and the CAW were stunned to discover that Buhler was advertising in Fargo for assemblers, welders, and mechanics at wage rates of between $8.50 and $15 an hour. Buhler owned thirty acres in the West Fargo Industrial Park, and Engel said a new tractor plant could be up and running by spring 2002. The new plant would only need about seventy-five workers to assemble the Genesis and Versatile tractors from parts that would be shipped in from Manitoba. The move, he said, was necessitated by the strike and by the Winnipeg plant being "grossly oversized."[4]

No one knew how seriously to take the threat—after all, Buhler had owned the land in Fargo for four years and advertising for workers a year before the plant was due to open seemed to be more of a bluff than a real recruiting plan. Economic development officials in Fargo appeared to be uncertain about the prospects. Only a few months earlier they had seen Case New Holland use a threatened move to Fargo to beat a concession out of UAW workers in Racine. Fargo-Cass County Economic Development officer Don Berg said, "Do we think it's for sure they are coming? No. Are we hopeful? Yes. Let's just say we are cautiously optimistic."[5]

Union president Rausch and McLaren drove down to Fargo to see how much substance there was to Buhler's threat of relocation. They dropped into the local CNH factory, presenting themselves as a pair of farmers interested in taking a plant tour. While they were going through the factory they asked questions about the local job market. They learned that Fargo was booming, that just that morning eleven people at the Case plant, all making $21 an hour, had quit. Later, with a smile Rausch recalled, "Buhler was offering between $9 and $15 per hour and these guys making $21 an hour quit and walked across the street and got jobs that paid just as well. What kind of people is he going to get? We knew that wasn't going to happen. He wouldn't be able to function there." McLaren noted that, unlike Versatile, CNH manufactured most of the parts for its tractors. The plant manager told him that the company had ended its contracting out policy because too often suppliers had not been able to meet their standards. McLaren said this had been the workers' experience at Versatile. McLaren and Rausch concluded that the threatened move could well have been a bluff.

Paterson said later that he probably changed his mind a hundred times about whether Buhler was serious about moving to North Dakota. "I think my overriding concept was he was bargaining, he had no intention of going, but you look awfully stupid if you made the wrong call.... So you had to negotiate, and you had to position yourselves for both eventualities." Paterson, not surprisingly, would have preferred more clarity in the negotiations.

> I'd rather have a company say, "We're going to close and we want to bargain a close-out agreement." I can deal with that. Or else the company says, "We're going to close, but you know what? If we can make the right deal, then we're prepared to stay." Then you can deal with that. But you can't deal with one where they're sending mixed signals to you. One minute he's staying, the next minute he's going. Then you say, "Let's look at the details of the loan. Wait a second here, there's nothing that says he has to continue operating in Canada. Holy shit, maybe he is going."

As soon as Buhler announced his intent to move to the United States, Paterson asked the CAW's national office to get him the background on the $32-million loan that had been transferred from New Holland to Buhler when he bought the plant. They were stunned to discover that there was no loan guarantee and no requirement for Buhler to maintain operations in Canada. Paterson passed the information on to NDP Member of Parliament Pat Martin and Liberal MP Reg Alcock, whose federal riding of Winnipeg South included the Versatile plant. Martin raised the issue in the house, while Alcock chose to ignore it. At one point McLaren led a march down to Alcock's constituency office, which was only a few blocks from the plant, to confront him about the loan. The meeting ended in an angry dispute over the nature and existence of the loan.

Manitoba government officials were also quick to criticize the federal government. Industry Minister MaryAnn Mihychuk wrote to federal Industry Minister Brian Tobin, saying, "I find it incomprehensible that your department would allow the company to assume this loan without requiring repayment if the company should leave the country."[6] After Lloyd Axworthy's retirement from federal politics in 2000, St. Boniface MP Ronald Duhamel had become the leading Manitoba Member of the federal government. He said he was distressed by Buhler's announcement, but could not see any way of stopping him from leaving the country. "To say that I'm disappointed is an understatement. We hope something can happen to turn it around. But there doesn't appear to be any legal requirement for the plant to stay in Canada."[7] Tobin took the position that his department had merely done what the Manitoba government had been asking it to do all along, namely to take every possible step to ensure that Buhler's bid to purchase Versatile succeeded.

With conciliation a failure and Buhler announcing that the company was no longer seeking arbitration, the provincial government's options were narrowing. On January 26 Labour Minister Becky Barrett appointed Wally Fox-Decent to serve as a mediator in the dispute. Fox-Decent, at the time the chairperson of the Manitoba Workers' Compensation Board, had become an all-round go-to guy for Manitoba governments of any political stripe. A Red Tory, Fox-Decent had lengthy and well-regarded careers in both the naval reserve, where he attained the position of rear admiral, and the academy, where he taught political studies at the University of Manitoba for thirty-two years. He had fallen into a labour relations side career when labour lawyer Mel Myers, whom he had known in university, asked him to serve as an arbitrator. Fox-Decent was reluctant at first, saying that he did not know the first thing about collective bargaining, but Myers persisted, arguing that he had the right abilities for the job. Over time Fox-Decent developed both a reputation as a skilled arbitrator of labour disputes and a public reputation for fairness. For this reason both NDP and Conservative governments passed on legislative hot potatoes to Fox-Decent on a regular basis: over the years he had headed task forces or reviews of the Meech Lake Constitutional Accord, national unity, Aboriginal child welfare, and remuneration of members of the legislative assembly. Fox-Decent was now given fifteen days to either end the dispute or come up with a report recommending a solution. At the time Buhler expressed relief at the appointment, saying, "Wally will be able to convey the truth. They don't understand we cannot provide job security."[8]

Fox-Decent held three meetings with both parties at the Charterhouse Hotel, but his efforts at mediating an agreement failed. The union was prepared to modify its proposals, but Buhler declined to give ground on seniority, benefits, and outsourcing. As Paterson commented to Fox-

Decent, "We seem to be bargaining with ourselves." At one point in the mediation process Buhler said he would not agree to binding arbitration until there was a return-to-work agreement. This was to prove to be one of the biggest stumbling blocks in resolving the dispute. Buhler wanted the right to choose the first fifty people who could return to work—and he wanted the right to choose them from not only the strikers but also the over four hundred people on layoff, all of whom had less seniority than the strikers. Furthermore he wanted the right to give these first fifty workers super seniority, which meant that his hand-picked workforce would never be subject to layoff. Since Buhler was talking about a vastly reduced workforce—he said his Fargo plant, for example, might only have seventy-five employees—he was asking for a return-to-work agreement that would allow him to make sure that very few, if any, of the strikers, ever returned to work. Such a proposal was not only unacceptable to the union, but also violated the provincial labour code, which stated that at the end of a strike workers should be recalled to the job on the basis of seniority. That Buhler was proposing the elimination of super seniority for the union bargaining team at that same time that he was proposing it for his hand-picked workforce was particularly provocative.

In his February 14 report Fox-Decent said that while the union and management were in disagreement on only a few issues, their differences on those points were significant. He concluded that the only way to end the strike and ensure the plant's future was for the two parties to agree to binding arbitration to settle the contract, any outstanding grievances, and—if the two parties could not quickly agree on a back-to-work protocol—a return-to-work agreement.

The union accepted Fox-Decent's recommendations on the day that the report was issued, although it was not an easy decision to reach. McLaren said the bargaining team "knew we had to do something."

> Standing outside was not an option. We knew our political careers were done at that point, but we thought we have to get these people back to work. We knew that people would not be happy with us. If we went to arbitration we were leaving ourselves open to having changes forced on us. It meant that there was a good chance that Fox-Decent was going to give Buhler some things we did not like and that we were not going to make any gains. But we also felt a responsibility to get people back to work.

Lussier recalled, "It was like pulling teeth for the other committee members to get me to go along with that decision." By agreeing to binding arbitration on both the return-to-work protocol and the contract itself, the union had reached a point of maximum flexibility. It was now prepared to put everything in the hands of a third party.

Buhler's immediate response to Fox-Decent's proposal was "not on your life." He said he would not recall workers unless the company got back the TV140 contract. Furthermore, he said he would not accept a return-to-work protocol that was based on seniority, and he apparently suspected that Fox-Decent would make seniority an element of any protocol that he imposed. Instead he still wanted the right to pick the first fifty workers to be recalled to work. The only solution, he said, was to leave Manitoba. "I have to go somewhere where there's right-to-work legislation."[9] Right-to-work legislation, which exists in North Dakota, undermines union security by allowing people to receive the benefits of a union contract without paying dues to the union. Two days later Engel formally rejected Fox-Decent's proposals. In his letter he argued that arbitration was no longer a solution because the company was now committed to moving to Fargo.

> We are truly saddened that the union did not see the merits of Binding Arbitration before it was too late to save the factory and jobs. The combination of: the loss of the TV140 contract; the reduced production of the other products due to the state of the industry; the extended time frame required to reestablish the supply chain, and; the nearing expiration of the sales agreement with CNH has meant that the factory cannot be justified. It is now over 4 times too large and inefficient. We now feel our best alternative is to protect the jobs of the salaried work force which has been able to maintain delivery of the Caterpillar product, and is training to begin producing Genesis and Versatile product at a significantly reduced rate until our new facility is ready.[10]

Buhler told the news media that he had offered to extend the conditions of work for two years. McLaren disputed this point, saying that reductions in seniority rights had always been on the table.

A despondent Fox-Decent reported, "What I know is that the strike should be over. Both sides should have said yes to my suggestions and one side didn't. There is nothing else, I fear, that can be done. This was a missed opportunity."[11]

For many of the bargaining committee members these developments were an important turning point in the strike. Mel Resler concluded that it was clear that Buhler did not intend to bring back most of the employees when he began demanding the right to pick the first fifty employees, and to include non-unionized workers who had been doing union work during the strike among them. Like other union members he doubted that Buhler intended to bring back much more than fifty workers in the near future—all of which meant that Resler had probably worked his last day in the Versatile plant. Rausch reached a similar conclusion. His wife asked him if he was considering quitting and he said, "No, I can't do that." As president of the Local he believed he should be the last to go. "I'm going to see this out, that's my job. That's what I got elected for and people are counting on. I'm staying until the last."

Buhler's decision to hire replacement workers heightened the tension on the picket line. As Joseph Smith recalled, "The workers were often provoked by people coming through the line, giving us the finger, telling us that, 'We have your jobs. We are working and you are not.'" These conflicts put different pressures on each member. However, no CAW members crossed the picket line. Ed Balik, who was far from being a union militant, explained:

> Why did no one cross the picket line? If somebody crossed, what could we do—kill him? No. But if you crossed the line, Buhler would destroy you, bringing down your wages, your benefits. He was offering only $1,000 in benefits per year per family. What is $1,000 today? You go to fix your teeth, a crown for one tooth costs you $600. No wonder he can afford to give money to the Health Science Centre. Since then I don't know if God exists if Buhler is such a believer in going to church.

When asked to recall his most striking memory in nine months as picket captain, John Pfeiffer said it was the lack of dissension. While he admitted that not everyone got along with everybody else—"there were people who you had a problem with in the plant"—after the strike got going they began to look at each other in a different light. "We all got along. There was not a harsh word between the guys on the line. There was no strife, or backstabbing." People weren't saying, "I'm doing more than him, go talk to him, get him to do it." McLaren said it was no accident that everyone on the line stuck together. "We orchestrated that, we held socials, we did a lot of campaigning, we had lots of meetings, we had social events, we had politicians come down and speak on the line."

Many of the strikers wanted to take the strike to Buhler's home and to the strikebreakers. Some members began to follow the strikebreakers home from work with the intent of leafleting their neighbourhoods or picketing their homes. According to McLaren, "Our members wanted to picket Buhler's home in the worst way. But there was no way that Dale or the national leadership would allow it." The CAW position was that a strike is a struggle that takes place at a workplace, and the union discouraged its members from moving the confrontation to people's homes. McLaren said he was under continual pressure to let the members expand the scope of the picketing, but held firm on this point. While the union worked hard to make sure that the members' anger did not bring them into conflict with the law, at times their frustration boiled over. Buhler, for example, said he received e-mails from the children of replacement workers who said that their father's tires had been slashed.[12]

In one case the strike pitted family members against one another. A long-time Versatile employee had arranged to get jobs for both of his sons at the plant. One son was a union member and participated in the strike. The other son had been a supervisor at the plant. He had left the company before to the start of the strike, but decided to return and work for the company during the strike. This led to conflict with both his father, who had retired from the company, and his brother, who planted signs in his brother's lawn denouncing him as a strikebreaker.

Angered by the lack of public support for the union, Dwight Pitcher's wife Cathy decided to do her part by writing letters to the editors of the *Winnipeg Free Press* and *Sun*. "Every time I opened the paper there was something in there," she said. "I would think, that is not what happened, that is not true." She was particularly incensed by the anti-union statements she kept seeing, day after day. "I am not a union member, but I just thought how can people have an opinion about something they are not involved in. I know what happened and how it happened." Dwight was worried that by taking on Buhler in public she would be putting her job as a financial adviser at the Bank of Nova Scotia at risk. But Cathy told her supervisor what she intended to do and even showed her the letter. The supervisor said as long as she was not bringing the bank or its clients into the conflict she could do what she wanted.

And so began a lengthy period of letter-writing. Pitcher wrote every time the strike was in the news or in response to comments that she heard on local talk shows. Every time a letter appeared in the paper it was put up on the wall of the strike trailer. According to Cathy, "People would say, I keep seeing your letters to the editor in the paper. Some pro-union said 'great' while others were not supportive. I told them that it was not a matter of being pro-union, it was being pro-Dwight and pro-us. It was my way of showing my support." Pitcher did not pull any punches. In one letter at the end of January she roasted Buhler along with all of the politicians involved in the dispute. She started off with a reference to the rally held in early 2000 at the International Inn, at which Premier Gary Doer, MP Reg Alcock, and Mayor Glen Murray had all voiced their support for the Versatile workers.

> Now, Premier Gary Doer does not want to get involved—so much for the party for labour. Maybe we could make Versatile a crown corporation, then we would all be rolling in money! Reg Alcock vowed not to let the tractor plant in his riding be closed. Now he wants nothing to do with it—he won't even return phone calls. So much for counting on your Member of Parliament. I guess he has his job for another four years so no need to worry about other people's jobs. Then there is Glen Murray—he's more concerned about garbage collection than jobs in his city. That shows where his priorities are.
>
> So where does this leave us? Out in the cold, literally. Over 240 workers on strike and over 100 workers laid off because John Buhler tells them that he has all the money and they can't have any of it. It's his way or the highway. Now it looks like he will be the one taking the highway—Highway 75 to Fargo that is. Looks like his promises are on par with promises from his government cohorts.[13]

Buhler said people who crossed the picket line would be offered jobs at his Fargo plant or in his Winnipeg operations. "I'll protect their jobs for the rest of my life. I'm going to reward somebody that works, not somebody that pickets." His promise of job security for replacement workers raised tempers on the picket line, especially given the strikers' awareness of his repeated comments that in today's economy there was no such thing as job security. Throughout the strike Buhler regularly commented that there was no way he could guarantee the workers job security because he could never tell how many tractors he would sell. It was, in a way, a non-issue: the CAW never asked for or expected that its members would be guaranteed work if the company was losing money. What the union was asking for was a guarantee that there be no contracting out of work, because contracting out eliminated jobs at the plant, and a guarantee that when workers were laid off, the most senior workers would be laid off last. No one would have complete job security, but the older workers would have more security than the younger workers. Employers can and do provide that sort of job security in thousands of unionized workplaces.

Buhler came under fire from all directions because he appeared to be about to skip town with $32 million of the taxpayers' money. Reform Party MP Brian Pallister, not a man normally hostile to members of the Manitoba business community, demanded to know what federal Industry Minister Tobin was going to do to prevent Buhler from walking off with the money. On the same day that Pallister was raising the issue, the Winnipeg Labour Council passed resolutions supporting the strike and calling on the government to prevent the plant from closing. New Democrat Pat Martin called Buhler's threat economic treason and demanded that "the government recall the loan before John Buhler steps across the border for Fargo, North Dakota, and save those jobs at Versatile Tractors for Canadians."[14] Paul Moist, the president of the Manitoba Region of the Canadian Union of Public Employees, wrote to the Manitoba NDP caucus urging it to make sure that Buhler felt the "full weight of government, should he continue with the tactics he had deployed to date."[15] Engel argued that all the company was doing was paying off someone else's loan. "We were not given a nickel of new money." He was, of course, conveniently ignoring how the loan reduced the amount of upfront money Buhler had to pay for the plant by $32 million.[16]

At a CAW think-tank in Mont-Tremblant, Quebec, Paterson once more put the case to the union leadership to let him lay unfair labour charges. The answer remained the same—fix it on the picket line, not with lawyers. But within a week the union changed its position as Hemi Mitic, now an assistant to CAW president Buzz Hargrove, gave Paterson permission to take Buhler to the Labour Board. Paterson did not lose any time. On February 23, 2001, the union filed an unfair labour practices charge. In making the charge, the CAW accused Buhler of:

- failing to bargain in good faith;
- failing to make every reasonable effort to reach a contract;
- failing to engage in full, rational, informed discussion about the issues;
- making patently unreasonable offers in collective bargaining (these, the union said, were designed to undermine the Local's status as a bargaining agent and coerce members into abandoning the union);
- pushing proposals to impasse;

- surface bargaining (a charge that implies the other party has only appeared to bargain without really intending on reaching an agreement).

After listing the number of bargaining sessions that had taken place, the union charged: "At the majority of the bargaining meetings set forth above, John Buhler alone has represented the Respondent. He has come to meetings unprepared and seemingly uninformed as to the critical issues between the parties in collective bargaining." The union pointed out several particularly unreasonable proposals: the dramatic reduction in benefits, the end of any limits on contracting out, and the changes to seniority.[17] It called on the Labour Board to order Buhler to bargain in good faith, to pay the CAW $900,000 to cover the cost of the strike, and to compensate the striking workers for their lost wages— $4.2 million by its estimate.

At the same time the CAW was filing this complaint with the Labour Board, Versatile strikers were engaged in a bit of street theatre outside the federal government's office of Western Economic Development. As a crowd of homeless people (portrayed by striking CAW members) were pepper-sprayed by mock RCMP officials, a Jean Chrétien look-alike (union member Frank Tangerdy) handed over bags of money to Stan Letwyn, who was dressed as Buhler, and Gary Kosheluk, who was portraying Engel. They then took the money, dumped it into the trunk of a waiting limousine–which had a "Fargo or bust" sign hanging off the licence plate—and drove off. Rausch told the media, "I think taxpayers shouldn't have to fund things going to the U.S. That money was earmarked for research and development, not to build another plant down in Fargo."[18]

Since the local's certification in 1985, Mel Myers had handled most of its legal work. However, in early 2001 Myers had been appointed head of the Manitoba Public Insurance Appeals Board. When he left private practice, he recommended that the union let Garth Smorang, a lawyer who had just started with his firm, Myers Weinberg, handle its legal work. When the CAW officials met with Smorang they were impressed, but they were also concerned that he might not fully understand the complexity of the issues. Paterson's view of Smorang was that the lawyer initially thought, "We'll lay the charge and hopefully they will go back to the table and settle." But the union said, "No, this goes a lot deeper than most charges of bargaining in bad faith." The union supplied Smorang with the notes from meetings, collected documents, the videos, news clips, everything that Buhler said publicly. McLaren recalled that while Smorang was happy to take on the case, he seemed doubtful that it would prove successful.

Smorang had acted on behalf of other unions, but had never before done a bad faith case. Indeed, this was only the third such case heard by the Manitoba Labour Board in twenty years. Smorang, though, had a strategy for proving that an employer has been bargaining in bad faith— which is to establish a motive for why the owner would carry out negotiations in that fashion:

> You'll never get the person to admit to bargaining in bad faith, so you have to rule out all other bona fide or legitimate business reasons for the way that they have bargained. In other words, if someone puts forward a proposal that says, "I need this from the union," then you have to literally go and investigate all of the reasons why [they need that] and try and figure out whether there is something that is legitimate. And if there is nothing legitimate, then all the Board is left with is the conclusion that there's an illegitimate reason.

Labour law draws a distinction between hard bargaining and bargaining in bad faith. There was nothing necessarily illegal or improper in any of the proposals that Buhler made—in the 1980s and 1990s many employers successfully bargained wage rollbacks, reductions in benefits, and changes in seniority. But, as Smorang explained, these proposals had to be linked to the company's economic health.

> Plenty of companies come to a union and say, "We've been losing money for the last three years and if we don't start making money this plant will close. And therefore I want you all to take a 10 per cent reduction in wages and benefits." If the union says to the company, "Fine, you say we've been losing money, let's see your financial statements," and the company says "No," then that is bad faith bargaining. If the company says "Okay," and shows them the financial statements and it's clear from the financial statements that the company has not been losing money, that's also bad faith bargaining.

Versatile was a viable manufacturer. It was not sold to Buhler because it was losing money but because it was, in effect, too successful and would give Case New Holland too large a share of the tractor market. Certainly the farm economy was in trouble, but that said nothing about the underlying financial viability of the company. Smorang said that both the content of Buhler's proposals and his style at the bargaining table smacked of bargaining in bad faith. "When you looked at his behaviour across the spectrum, in other words from the first meeting, then how did it change at the second meeting and what position did he take at the third meeting and how did that follow through to the fourth meeting, etc." According to Smorang, Buhler's position through the attempted negotiations revealed definite patterns that neatly matched the criteria for bad faith bargaining.

But the question remained, "What was Buhler's motive?" Smorang said that he never thought for a moment that Buhler was a stupid man, which gave rise to a key question: why, if, as reported, he paid close to $100 million for a company, would he have let the workers go on strike for so long and lost the TV140 contract? It all made no sense to Smorang. "I couldn't understand why he would buy a plant, sit down at a few reasonably brief bargaining sessions without accountants, without lawyers, without other people around him, and bargain almost off the cuff. Why would he let his employees go on strike and let that strike ruin his business to the point where he was now saying 'I have to move this business out of the country?" Perhaps Buhler intended all along to move the company out of the country, in which case he would be guilty of bargaining in bad faith. Or, perhaps, Smorang thought, "We're not getting the straight goods on the price of the firm."

The only theory that made sense was the one that McLaren and Rausch had been promoting since the fall: namely, that Buhler had been given a sweetheart deal with the expectation that he would not be able to keep the plant viable. Other people were also starting to raise questions about how much Buhler had actually paid for Versatile. *Free Press* business reporter Martin Cash noted that a close reading of Buhler's annual report suggested that Buhler had paid far less "than the published reports of $100 million to $150 million for the Fort Garry plant." To his credit Cash added, "The *Free Press* was as guilty as the rest in reporting that inflated number." According to Cash, it now looked as if Buhler had spent no more than $15 million for the company.[19]

Smorang looked not only at Buhler's bargaining style during the strike, but also at the events surrounding the loss of the TV140, the conditions on the loan, and the threat to move to Fargo. He began to formulate a theory based on McLaren and Rausch's interpretation of the deal. Like them, Smorang concluded that Buhler may well have gone to the bargaining table intending to reach an impasse and provoke a strike.

As Smorang put it, "Normally, the employer needs to bargain in good faith to ensure that production continues. But if you did not pay anything for the plant and are thinking of moving it to Fargo, then you do not have an incentive to bargain."

Three days after the union laid the unfair labour charges, Buhler and Paterson squared off in a debate sponsored by the Labour Studies program at the University of Manitoba. Given the participants it was a surprisingly low-key affair. Buhler and Paterson each made brief comments and then, instead of mixing it up with one another, took questions from the audience, many of whom were striking Versatile members. In his opening statement Buhler stressed that in November he had offered to take the dispute to binding arbitration and the union had turned him down. This was, by far, the strongest card that he had to play. In addressing the other issues he said that job security had to be earned, not negotiated—ignoring that the striking workers had presumably earned their job security over the twenty years or more that each of them had put in at the plant.

Buhler tried to make the case that the plant was a money-loser, pointing out that it had nearly gone bankrupt in the 1980s and New Holland had made only three payments on its loan to the federal government over the thirteen years of the loan's existence. When Paterson pointed out that since New Holland had not been required to make any payments for ten years, and furthermore was not required to make payments in years when the company lost money, it would appear that the plant had made money in each of the last three years, since New Holland had made payments in each of those years. Buhler's final message, however, was that the factory was closed—it could not operate without the TV140 contract.

While Buhler was cautious about what he said during the debate, he did make a number of revealing observations. He indicated that the provincial government was still trying to salvage the TV140 contract, which suggests that even at that late date the contract was not necessarily cancelled. When he was asked why he had demanded that there be no requirement in the loan that he maintain production in Canada, he said, "If there had been any conditions on that loan, I would have been forced to give the union whatever they wanted," a statement that implied the move to the United States had been in the back of his mind even before he bought the plant. As to what should happen to the workers, he said, "The provincial government should buy the plant and keep you working." This was an idea that would re-emerge in coming weeks.

The *Free Press* editorial board used the strike and the unsecured loan to take a swipe at former Liberal cabinet minister Axworthy for having supported Buhler's purchase of the plant, arguing that Canada should have accepted the U.S. Justice Department position that Buhler Industries was not large enough to take over Versatile and compete internationally.

> The Versatile workers and the Fort Garry property might by now have found work with a future if nature had been allowed to take its course. Lloyd Axworthy, however, decided that Buhler Industries would be the saviour of Versatile. Winnipeg and Manitoba are now stuck with the painful and unproductive results of his choices.
>
> It is too late to unmake those choices. There will, however, be time to recall them when the next failing industry comes forward seeking help from the government.[20]

It is of, course, the editorialist's role to come down from the hills after the battle and kill the wounded, but it is worth noting that over the years the *Winnipeg Free Press* had printed many articles extolling the importance of the Versatile plant to the Manitoba economy. Axworthy may have been mistaken for thinking of Buhler as a miracle turnaround artist, but it was also a mistake that had been propounded in many *Free Press* profiles of the entrepreneur. More significantly, the line of thought misrepresents the farm equipment industry—it may have been in a downturn, but as long as there is a market for bread it remains an industry with a future. The editorial also makes it clear that a key element of the city's establishment was prepared to see the city de-industrialized without putting up a fight. The leaders of Local 2224 thought the real problem was too little, not too much, government involvement. In the coming weeks the union would mount an intense campaign that would underscore the provincial government's inability or unwillingness to intervene in a manner that would force Buhler to abandon his plans to move to the United States and to bargain in good faith with the union.

9

Cowboy Capitalists and Labour-Friendly Governments

A Long March

In the University of Manitoba debate, Buhler had stated publicly that there was no point to continued negotiations with the CAW because he intended on closing the plant and moving production to the United States. The workers' only hope, he said dismissively, was to have the provincial government buy the plant. The CAW decided to take Buhler up on that idea.

The previous year, while lobbying the provincial government to take steps to protect the pension plan, Dale Paterson had encouraged Premier Doer to consider having the province take an equity position in the company to protect the jobs and their technology. With Buhler's talk of plant closure and there being no guarantee of protection for the federal government's investment, in the spring of 2001 the Local leadership began to focus on the case for a government takeover—a case that seemed stronger than ever. Even if the strategy did not succeed, the thought that the government might buy him out could lead Buhler to make an acceptable offer. Both Len Rausch and Scott McLaren had been long-time members of the New Democratic Party in Doer's Concordia riding. They had both served on the riding executive. During the strike they met several times not only with Labour Minister Barrett, but with senior government officials including Eugene Kostyra, the secretary of the Cabinet Committee on Community and Economic Development. In these meetings they began to lobby for the province to take over the plant, at least until a new buyer could be found.

The idea of a government takeover of the Versatile plant did not receive a warm welcome. While the Doer government recognized the importance of the Versatile plant, it had never exhibited any interest in nationalizing manufacturing enterprises, even on a temporary basis. On the contrary: during the previous year's debate over changes to the labour code the NDP administration had shown itself to be remarkably sensitive to criticism from the business community to the effect that it was pandering to the interests of organized labour. As a result the government had actually modified what had been a fairly modest set of proposals to begin with. Any steps to take over Versatile would leave Doer open to charges of bailing out both the CAW and a failing plant—indeed, the *Free Press* had already made its opposition to such a move abundantly clear.

Many CAW members pointed out how in the 1970s the NDP government of Ed Schreyer had taken over a number of manufacturing concerns, including the Flyer Industries bus company and the Churchill Forest Industries (CFI) complex in The Pas. The union members argued that the government had been able to provide support for these industries until they could be sold back to the private sector. In fact, Flyer and CFI had fallen into the Schreyer government's hands largely by accident. The previous Conservative government had made numerous financial loans and commitments to these firms—and then, as they failed, the government ended up as owner by default. Through the Manitoba Development Corporation (MDC), the Schreyer government ended up owning a range of commercial enterprises, including CFI, Flyer, Saunders Aircraft, and Morden Fine Foods. While these operations made a contribution to the provincial economy, many of them were money-losing ventures. In his memoirs, Sidney Green, the Schreyer government cabinet minister responsible for MDC, awkwardly concluded, "The Schreyer government attempted with less success than failure to have funds advanced on a sound financial basis."[1] Len Evans, the minister responsible for the Manitoba Development Corporation when the government took over Flyer, said that Manitoba was starving for jobs when it took over the company and pointed out that the company was still in the business of employing people. He also recognized that for the NDP, "The political costs of taking over these plants outweighed the economic benefit. People do not allow government to lose money. It is not unusual for a private company to lose money for three or four years in its early years of operation. Government-owned firms are not granted that much leeway." The money lost by firms like Flyer was a serious political liability that contributed to Schreyer's defeat in 1977.

During the 1980s, when Eugene Kostyra was Howard Pawley's minister of economic development, and responsible for Flyer, he concluded that a small provincial government had no business owning a company that had to compete in a technologically evolving international market. As a result, he sold Flyer to a Dutch-based firm. The Pawley government also attempted to nationalize the private natural gas utility in the mid-1980s, but unresolved concerns over potential tax liability scuttled the deal. (Strangely enough, in the 1990s, when he was busy privatizing many government operations, Conservative Premier Gary Filmon nationalized the gas utility.)

In opposition Doer had fought Filmon's decision to sell off the Manitoba Telephone System (MTS), and later, as premier, he brought in legislation requiring a referendum prior to any privatization of Manitoba Hydro. Still, he now recognized that the public was suspicious of NDP-initiated business ventures, and as a very cautious politician—and owing much of his success to that caution—he was unlikely to offer the business community, the Conservatives, and the *Free Press* such an easy target.

On March 1, 2001, 250 CAW members took their street theatre to the steps of the Manitoba legislature. Each striker had made a cardboard tombstone listing his start date, job title, and years of seniority. Mounted on wooden stakes, these signs were planted on the grounds of the legislature. The display constituted an eerie graveyard of unemployment and broken futures, spreading out from the front steps of the legislature to Broadway.

When Barrett addressed the cold and angry crowd that morning, she told them: "Mr. Buhler saying that he doesn't understand the concept of seniority or concept of benefits or even the concept of the right to strike can't possibly be accurate. Seniority and benefits are two of the mainstays of the labour movement. Mr. Buhler cannot plead ignorance of the labour movement." While the labour minister is expected to maintain a neutral role in a labour dispute, Barrett approvingly quoted Wally Fox-Decent's comment that the strike was continuing because one party—Buhler—had refused to agree to arbitration. She received a positive response from the union members, but as he thanked her for her comments Rausch remarked that the union would like to see the government bring in legislation banning the use of strikebreakers and protecting workers' rights in the event of a plant closure.

In the previous session of the legislature the NDP had adopted changes to the labour code that allowed it to impose binding arbitration to end lengthy strikes; but that legislation had not come into effect until after the start of the Versatile strike. The CAW now called on the NDP to apply that law retroactively to its strike. Speaking on behalf of the government, Barrett did not agree to making legislative changes immediately, but said she was not closing the door.[2] While the CAW was able to point to a number of examples of governments making labour legislation retroactive, such legislative changes are rare and would certainly have opened up the NDP to charges of catering to the CAW; and they would also have stood a good possibility of being struck down by the courts.

CAW national president Buzz Hargrove arrived in town the next day, determined to convince Buhler not to move the factory. If Buhler refused to budge, Hargrove told the news media, the federal and provincial governments should take over the plant. "We want a relationship with him, but if Mr. Buhler doesn't want to operate this thing, I think the government ought to take it over and nationalize it." Hargrove later recalled the meeting with Buhler in a room at the downtown Fairmont Hotel as the most unusual, and unproductive, meeting in his career as a union leader. First of all, Buhler and Engel were both accompanied by their wives. "It was so peculiar, so out of stride. Buhler brought a digital camera, he wanted a photo with me for his collection of pictures of prominent people." Because he was hoping to get along with the owner, Hargrove posed for a photo with Buhler. He then said to him "I have an idea that will make you a lot of money. Let's end this strike, get people back to work, building tractors." According to Hargrove, Buhler looked at him and said, "I hope you did not come here thinking we can find an agreement. That is not going to happen. We are closing we are moving to North Dakota." Eventually Hargrove, concluding that there was no way he could convince Buhler to change his mind, broke off the meeting.

The following morning's paper reported Hargrove's call for nationalization, as well as what appeared to be the Doer government's immediate rejection of the idea. According to the paper, "A senior assistant to the premier last night dismissed the notion out of hand." The official remarked that it was "unfortunate" that Hargrove had "thrown out that as a pressure tactic, but it's just not in the cards." The official reportedly argued that the province could not "justify taking over a private business because of a labour dispute."[3]

The Doer government's rejection came as no surprise to Hargrove— prior to meeting with Buhler, Hargrove had dined with Barrett, who told him the government had no interest in taking over the plant. Under Hargrove's leadership the CAW had developed a particularly hard-edged love-hate relationship with both the federal and Ontario NDP. Few unions put more money or resources into supporting the NDP than did the CAW. At the same time Hargrove could be one of the party's most vocal critics. During the 1990s in particular the CAW clashed with Bob

Rae's NDP government in Ontario. No one was surprised when he responded aggressively to the NDP decision not to even consider taking over the plant. At a news conference the next morning Hargrove renewed his call for the federal and provincial governments to hire independent consultants to evaluate the firm, and then purchase it from Buhler based on that price. Hargrove stressed that he was not asking the Manitoba government to bail the CAW out of a labour-relations problem. "This is not a labour dispute. This is a cowboy capitalist who has made the decision to move these jobs out of the country." Hargrove pointed out that over the years both the federal and provincial governments had made significant investments in what was a world-class plant, making this a "a fight about capital and its responsibility to the community," not simply a fight between an employer and a union. It was the perfect time for government action because the workers "don't need government when things are going well." It was government's role to step in during a crisis. It was a controversial call, one designed to dramatically increase the level of attention being paid to the dispute.

At Local 2224's membership rally in a ballroom in the Fairmont Hotel that day, Hargrove expressed his anger with the Doer government for its apparent out-of-hand rejection of his proposal. He would have fired any aide of his who acted in the way that the government representative quoted by the *Free Press* did, he said. Hargrove added:

> NDP members often come up to me and ask, "Why are the unions voting for the other parties?"... I tell them that government is about providing a counterbalance to corporate power, especially the abuses of this power.... The federal government already has $31 million in it. The province already has money in it. Now are we going to sit back and allow a private entrepreneur to say: "I don't care about that; I'm going to move the thing out of the country?" When Gary Filmon was premier, he never failed to step in for the interests of business.... Well it's not good enough for the NDP to say: "We are the government of labour" and not act.[4]

In her comments at that day's rally Barrett did not refer to the possibility of nationalization, while NDP MP Pat Martin came out in favour of the federal government buying Versatile as an interim measure until a new owner could be recruited. Before the meeting broke up the CAW members and their supporters passed resolutions calling on the federal and provincial governments to take over the plant. It also called on the province to pass plant-closure legislation that would provide for fair treatment of employees, including notice and severance provisions and legislation that would end the strike and impose binding arbitration.

Relations between the NDP and CAW did not improve. Buhler said he would happily sell the plant to the government if it wanted to pay between $50 and $100 million. But Industry Minister Mihychuk was not biting at any price. "There's no intention on behalf of this government to get into this dispute by nationalizing a tractor company."[5] The following day Hargrove said,

> If the government of Manitoba, an NDP government, dismisses this out of hand, they can be assured that they've lost the support of our union locally and nationally. If that's what an NDP government means for working people, then there's not much reason for us to support the NDP.... If the NDP can't step in there, then there's absolutely no question I will recommend across the country that we withdraw our support completely from the NDP.

The *Free Press* editorialized against any nationalization, as did reporter Martin Cash, who dismissed it as a loopy scenario: "What seems perhaps to be the only justice in the piece is that these two sides deserve each other."[6]

Although he continued to oppose buying the plant, Doer branded Buhler's decision to relocate as "the most anti-community activity I could ever witness," while St. Boniface's Liberal MP Ronald Duhamel said that morally Buhler ought to pay back the loan before leaving. Buhler defended himself by saying that he had put between $50 million and $100 million into the plant since taking it over.[7] For its part, the CAW continued to urge the government to take over the plant. Mounting a letter-writing campaign, CAW members pointed to the way the Ontario NDP government of Bob Rae had stepped in to prevent the closure of de Havilland Aircraft in 1992. The company had since been acquired by Bombardier and was operating successfully. Smarting from the characterization that it had rejected the CAW's original nationalization proposals "out of hand," the NDP became somewhat more diplomatic. Government communications director Donne Flanagan told the press, "There are reasonable limits to what a government can or ought to do when it comes to a private company. If the CAW has reasonable options for us to look at, we will obviously be there."[8]

The arguments for keeping the plant in Manitoba were as strong as they had been the year before. Even when the plant was down to the current 250 unionized workers it created an additional 450 spin-off jobs in the Manitoba economy. Just counting the existing workforce, Winnipeg would lose 700 jobs if Buhler were allowed to move the plant. The provincial and federal governments would lose $10 million in income and sales tax revenue. Furthermore, the interest-free nature of the loan to Buhler amounted to a $12-million subsidy from the federal government to the company. Given these figures, the CAW argued that the governments should buy the company for $10 million—the $15 million they estimated that Buhler paid for the company minus the $5 million in wages the CAW members had lost during the strike. According to the union plan:

> After buying back the facility from Buhler, the two levels of government would seek out a new private sector partner to operate the facility, using the licensed technology that came with the plant. This new partner could work into an equity position in the operation by supplying working capital and technology, and would eventually become majority owner as the plant's financial prospects improved.

According to the union, this was not a bailout.

> The underlying economic conditions of the Versatile plant are good. It produces tractors which are well-regarded for their quality, and are priced competitively. The lack of competition in the agricultural implements industry means that Versatile's competitive presence is needed more than ever. Versatile is not a "basket case" seeking government aid; it is a healthy enterprise being destroyed by ideological mismanagement.[9]

Buhler replied that he would never sell the company for the $10 million recommended by the union, asking a reporter, "If you paid $90 million for something, would you sell it for $10 million?"[10] In response CAW economist Jim Stanford pointed out that Buhler Industry documents stated that for the year ending in September 2000 the company's capital expenditures totalled $18 million and that the firm had indicated "the bulk of this amount" was a result of the tractor factory acquisition. Stanford concluded, "This would imply that the capital cost to Buhler Industries of the acquisition was something less than $18 million." While the annual report showed a $32-million increase in inventory, most likely accounted for by the Versatile inventory, Stanford pointed out that this increase was offset by the $32-million loan.[11] Engel joined in with a letter to Stanford, saying "that if the sale of the tractor operation was contemplated between Buhler Versatile Inc. and a suitable buyer ... all pertinent information would be provided as part of the traditional due diligence proceedings between the parties."[12]

The relations between the Doer government and the CAW were further complicated by an internal conflict in the Canadian labour movement. In February 2000, eight large Ontario locals of the Service Employees International Union voted to leave the SEIU and join the CAW. Hargrove said the merger was an example of workers deciding their own future in a free and democratic fashion. The leaders of the SEIU, a US-based union, called it a raid and took their complaints to the Canadian Labour Congress (CLC). Both the CAW and the SEIU, along with many other unions that operate in Canada, were members of the CLC. In theory each CLC affiliate is supposed to have an exclusive jurisdiction; the CAW has auto workers, the Canadian Union of Postal Workers has Canada Post employees, the Steelworkers has miners and steel workers, and so on. Unions are expected to stick to their jurisdiction and not engage in what might be seen as divisive conflicts. In reality, almost from the beginning no union has ever stuck solely to its own jurisdiction. Bernard Christophe, for years the leader of the United Food and Commercial Workers in Manitoba, used to joke that if a worker ate meat they were in his jurisdiction. In response to the SEIU-CAW dispute the CLC prohibited the CAW from participating in Congress events, a ban that effectively expelled the union from the Congress. It also had the effect of expelling the union from the various provincial federations of labour, including the Manitoba Federation of Labour (MFL). The conflict soured relations between many provincial union leaders and the CAW in Manitoba and across the country. It also led some to interpret Local 2224's call for the nationalization of the plant as a part of the CAW's ongoing conflict with the CLC and NDP. The split in Manitoba was far from clear-cut, however. Paul Moist, the president of the Manitoba Division of the Canadian Union of Public Employees, was a visible supporter of Local 2224 even though Hargrove and CUPE national president Judy Darcy had clashed on a number of occasions over the CAW's merger with the SEIU locals. Furthermore two senior MFL officials attended Local 2224's March 3 rally at the Fairmont Hotel.

Hemi Mitic, Paterson, and the Local 2224 members met with the NDP caucus on April 9, once more asking the government to take action to save an important industry. Mitic pointed out that the workers were also likely to lose their severance pay if Buhler moved the plant across the border, adding that the CAW did not want to get into the same sort of confrontation that had developed between the labour movement and the NDP in Ontario when Rae was premier in the early 1990s. But, he said, "We are feeling lonely out there." In his opinion this was an opportunity for government to "be smart and controversial.... You can make this a potential issue and secure the jobs in the long term." He told the government that they had to make it clear to Buhler that a price would be paid for going down the road.

In his response Doer stressed that no one in the room was happy. He pointed out that Rausch was the chair of his constituency organization and a long-time supporter. The government, he said, had put a lot of effort into keeping the plant in Winnipeg, but clearly the "union was not on Buhler's dance card." Doer said he believed that Buhler was too concerned about his local image to move the plant, but recognized that his actions were difficult to predict. Though the government was open to some sort of bridging arrangement to keep the plant open, there had to be other partners. Finally, he said the government had tried everything it could to have some influence on Buhler. While he recognized the risks faced by the men on strike, he also had to admit, "We haven't a solution. I don't want to create any false impressions."

For Mitic, waiting for another partner was simply not good enough. He said the federal government kept asking, "What's your government [meaning the NDP government] doing?" The solution, he said, had to start in that caucus room. He said the CAW had handed the government an issue, which was to protect the jobs of working Manitobans. McLaren told Doer, "This plant can produce more than just tractors. This government should be embarrassed if it doesn't make the first move."

Doer concluded the meeting by thanking the delegation for an honest discussion, saying the government would not be taking any action until the Labour Board hearings had ended.

The union members held a barbecue at the legislature the next day, but spirits were not high. Rausch pointed out that in 1990, when Varta Batteries closed, Doer, then in opposition, had called for plant-closing legislation. At the time Doer had said, "Manitoba is rapidly gaining the reputation as the easiest place in Canada to close a plant. The Premier [at the time, Filmon] must develop a strategy to deal with the ever-increasing number of plant closures in this province. Failure to do so will result in a further decline in our manufacturing base." Since taking power the NDP had not brought in any such legislation, leaving it one of the few provinces in Canada without such a law.[13]

The debate over plant-closing legislation dated back to the early 1980s. Prior to the recession of 1982 the Manitoba manufacturing sector had experienced decades of regular growth. But from 1981 to 1987 the sector lost 9,000 jobs. Nor did the economic recovery of the late 1980s end this trend. The period of 1976 to 1990 in Manitoba saw 114 closures involving fifty or more employees for a total job loss of 14,957. More than a third of those closures were the result of corporate restructurings, which usually saw out-of-province owners close profitable operations and relocate production. In a number of cases out-of-province competitors simply bought Manitoba plants and shut them down. These shutdowns had led to the increased labour interest in plant-closing legislation. Such legislation would require employers to provide a lengthy notice of their intent to shut down, allow for a public review of the plant's viability, and determine if the plant could continue to operate under a new owner. During the 1981 provincial election the New Democratic Party had promised to introduce legislation to make it harder for employers to close down plants. Once in office, however, the NDP limited itself to requiring a longer notice period prior to a shutdown and providing the labour minister with the power to establish an industrial adjustment committee in the event of a shutdown. The fear at the time was that too aggressive an approach to plant-closing would simply drive away future private investment.[14]

Members of the Doer government were not happy to see CAW members protesting at the legislature on the same day that the government was bringing in its second budget. Nor was the public criticism of the NDP improving the relations between the CAW and other unions affiliated to the Manitoba Federation of Labour. A sore point for many members of Local 2224 was that other union leaders walked silently past their demonstration in front of the legislature on their way to hear the budget speech. Stan Letwyn spoke of it as crossing their picket line.

On a national level a mild thawing of relations took place between the CAW and CLC. Congress president Ken Georgetti wrote to federal Industry Minister Tobin urging him to "intervene on behalf of the federal government to save 2,000 jobs in the Winnipeg area."[15] Pat Martin called on the federal government to demand full payment from Buhler if he moved to Fargo: "We can't let John Buhler slip across the border with $32 million in taxpayers' money, to create jobs in Fargo North Dakota.... When a contract is silent or ambiguous, an arbitrator looks to what was the original intent of the two parties. Do you think it was our intent to create jobs in Fargo?"[16] As late as mid-May Rausch and McLaren met with several former senior Versatile managers, engineers, and superintendents to see if they were prepared to support the idea of a government purchase of the plant. The case for a government takeover would be stronger, they believed, if an experienced interim management committee was at the ready, waiting in the wings. The people at the meeting were unhappy at the direction Buhler had taken the company, and several indicated that they would be prepared to support a bid to take over the plant. However, due to a lack of government interest in taking over the plant, the group never met again and no formal proposal was developed. The union's future was now in the Labour Board's hands.

The hearings began on Monday, March 19. Buhler's lawyer, Tracey Epp, told the Board, "I'm the first to admit, and the evidence will show, that Mr. Buhler has a completely different bargaining style from that which this local is accustomed to. That doesn't make it bargaining in bad faith, it just makes it different." In outlining the CAW's case Garth Smorang stated, "This strike happened because the employer wanted it to happen, intended it to happen, and for business reasons, had profited from it happening."

Paterson was the first witness, testifying that from the start of the talks it appeared as if Buhler was taunting the union, going after benefits, seniority, and severance.[17] While the hearings were expected to continue the next day, Chuck McCormick, the employee appointee on the Labour Board, came down with a sudden illness, forcing an adjournment until at least until mid-April.

The strike had now been on for five months. While the CAW members remained united in their rejection of Buhler's proposals, they were suffering economically. Some, like Louis Mora, who was working a night shift at a McDonald's restaurant, had been forced to seek other jobs. As Richard Ullmann said, "There were probably a lot of people there that lived from pay cheque to pay cheque. There weren't a lot of people that had a lot of savings." A few weeks before the strike started, Ullmann's wife, Sherry, had enrolled in a health-care-aide training program. She had to deal with the stress of going back to school and worries over the family's finances. Each night she would read aloud to Richard the material that she was preparing for her schoolwork—it must have helped, because she graduated at the top of her class, but Richard wondered how much assistance he really gave her. "It must have been like reading to a blank wall at times."

Sherry was outraged by Buhler's approach to negotiations. "I did not think it was right to come in, slap the guys in the face, and say, 'I am the new boss, this is what you had and this is what I am giving you.' He was taking everything away from them that the union had got for them over the years." Like a number of other families, the Ullmanns cancelled their subscription to the *Winnipeg Sun*. According to Sherry, "We were tired of seeing the union trashed every day."

Ray Wilkie said, "If it was not for my wife working and my having good credit, I would have lost everything. You try to live off $200 a week when you're used to $500 a week." Wilkie's wife had to postpone her planned retirement for two years to make up for the financial damage that the family experienced during the strike. Her brother, who also worked at Versatile, lost his house. Bill Sokoliuk said, "My family took a lot of shellacking. Whatever I had saved I used to have to take out because things weren't going right." Ed Balik's wife, in her late fifties, had to take a job to help the family make ends meet. Both of Sandy Brar's children were in university during the strike. "We were in very bad shape. My wife was making $10 an hour. That would put food on the table, but what about the mortgage, books, and tuition?"

The strike was a bleak time for Winston Johnson's family. His two children were also in university, and the family had mortgage payments to make. His wife worked at a personal care home in St. Norbert and was forced to take extra shifts to help out. The family stood firm in their resolve not to give up just because they were going through a tough time. One month into the strike Johnson came across an attractive job opportunity, but he turned it down—that would not have been, he said, "fair to the people" he had "stood side by side and worked with."

> So I held out, I held my ground like everybody else. Some people went and found jobs, but most people in the leadership did not. Because if the members see you running they think something is up. They think, "if the leadership is looking for work then we're wasting our time." So we had to demonstrate leadership by not going out there and looking for work.

While no CAW members ever crossed the picket line, the strike was not without its internal stresses. At one point Joseph Smith found himself in an argument with one of the old Hydraulic Engineering Workers Association supporters, who said the union should have accepted the company offer. Smith told him that was why the workers had thrown the Association out years ago: "Anything the company would offer you would take. You didn't have the guts to stand up and say no." Letwyn was worried that some members would take out their frustration on the management employees who had allowed Buhler to maintain production. "I figured that someone would have got hurt or killed. Some of these guys had stolen our jobs and worked and caused us so much pain. Some people lost their houses, cars, stuff like this, you know, couldn't put their kids in university. I had to cash in RRSPs. I had to sign away my life insurance."

The leadership held the Labour Board hearing out to the members as a way of bringing the strike to an end, and picket captains like Wilkie used the Labour Board complaint to keep spirits up. "I would talk to people on the line and remind them that we had won at the Labour Board in the past. I had to take a lot of heat from people who said we would not win. But I remained confident."

Now it appeared that workers would have to wait months for a Labour Board decision. Faced with the delay, the union leadership came up with a startling proposal—ending the strike without an agreement.

The idea was Hemi Mitic's. According to Manitoba labour law, "a legal strike ends on the date on which the union which was the bargaining agent for the employees in the unit at the time the strike commenced indicates in writing to the employer that the strike is over." The *Labour Relations Act* also states that at the end of a strike, if there is no other agreed upon arrangement, workers must be recalled "as work becomes available on the basis of the seniority standing of the employee in relation to the seniority of the other employees in the unit employed at the time the lockout or strike commenced." Furthermore, once the union has ended the strike the employer cannot continue to employ replacement workers and refuse to bring back striking workers. Buhler would also have to lay off those strikers whom he did not need at that time, allowing them to collect unemployment insurance benefits. These were the potential benefits to the CAW of calling off the strike.

The downside was simple—no one was certain as to what the terms and conditions of work would be when they returned or how they would be able, after that, to pressure Buhler into negotiating a satisfactory agreement. Finally there was the very real question as to whether or not Buhler would let the strikers back into the plant. If, as the union had come to suspect, Buhler had no intention of operating Versatile as a large-scale tractor plant, the last thing he wanted was an end to the strike. He might retaliate by locking them out. If he did, he would have made it clear that it was his intransigence, not the union's, that was prolonging the dispute. Until that point he had made a number of public statements indicating that he would never lock the union out. If Buhler was not careful, a lockout could trigger new unfair labour practice charges.

The CAW had taken such a strategy once before in Manitoba, in

1981, when its members were on strike at Boeing. The morale was low and the company had sent out a letter instructing the strikers to return to work. Mitic was working for the union at the time, and during a membership meeting at the Assiniboine Hotel he concluded that the strike was failing. To prevent the strike from collapsing on the union, he proposed that the workers end it and return to work directly from the hotel. The union agreed, went back to work, and as a result salvaged a modest agreement and saved the local. As Mitic put it, "You've got to do anything in this racket, otherwise you can get killed."

The CAW proposal along that line would in essence set a trap for Buhler. He would either have to lock the workers out or, with no return-to-work agreement in place, take the workers back in order of seniority. But under Manitoba law an employer cannot lock out workers unless the company has placed a complete offer on the table—and Buhler had yet to table a complete offer. Both of Buhler's options at this point must have seemed unpalatable: a lockout would probably lead to further unfair labour practice charges, recalling workers on the basis of seniority would mean that forfeiting his ability to pick and choose his workforce.

McLaren thought the membership might revolt against the leadership for even proposing a return to work without a contract. He told Mitic, "This is not something the membership is going to like. They are dug in. We are there every day, rallying the troops. To turn and retreat—and it will be perceived that way, they will say we are selling them out." The leaders also had another problem: they could not tell the members that they expected Buhler to illegally lock them out if they agreed to return to work, because word of that plan might get back to Buhler. Mitic assured McLaren that they would be able to sell the idea, but it was with serious reservations that the bargaining committee chair agreed to take the proposal to the members on Sunday, March 25.

The response was negative. As Paterson recalled, the members thought "we had all lost our minds." Many of the members were dumfounded. Sokoliuk could not believe it when he heard that the union was going to recommend a return to work. He argued that Buhler would "never accept us. Maybe he'll take us but you know he might have all kind of rules." Mora said that to vote an end to the strike was to admit defeat, and he voted against the proposal. He worried, "If Buhler was smart he would simply lay everybody off. We were gambling with everybody's future." Wilkie recalled that McLaren virtually had to beg the members to vote to end the strike. "It was a very, very, very, very touchy thing to do." Wilkie worried that Buhler would accept the workers back but lay most of them off for lack of work.

Lussier supported the decision, confident that Buhler would not let the union back in the plant. "Buhler was worried because there had been a lot of animosity on the picket line, and he was worried about letting the inmates back in. We knew full well that he wasn't going to accept it. There ain't no way he was going to let us back in the plant." Letwyn agreed. "We never ever thought in our wildest dreams that Buhler would let us go back. We thought he'd just keep burying himself deeper. But if we did go back everybody would have their job for a while."

McLaren told the members that the bargaining team recognized that it was asking the members to take a leap of faith. But, he said, the union did have a plan. In the end the vote to end the strike, which was in essence a tremendous show of confidence in the local leadership, was passed by 148 to 31. Later that day Paterson faxed Buhler a message indicating that the union was calling off the strike and wanted to meet to discuss a return to work.

Buhler and Engel were just as shocked by this turn of events as the union members had been by the proposal to return to work. Engel would later state that, at the time, he believed the union had accepted the company's last proposal—although there was no mention of such acceptance in the letter. The confusion of the owner and his representative was apparent on the following day, when Engel told Mitic that he could recall about fifteen employees a week for about six weeks but would not do so based on seniority. In other words, the two parties were still at loggerheads over the return-to-work agreement. Mitic told him that if the company did not call workers back based on seniority, according to the law, the union would file an unfair labour practice charge.[18]

Meanwhile McLaren was praying that Buhler and Engel would take the bait and lock the union out. "I was absolutely distraught because I was not at all certain he would do it. If he didn't, I would be the one who had to take responsibility for having told the people to trust us and our plan." Late on March 27 his prayers were answered. Engel informed Paterson that the company was locking the workers out until a new contract and return-to-work agreement could be reached. He asked that Fox-Decent resume his work as a mediator.[19] Engel told reporters, "Unfortunately for me, to build tractors today with management people, I needed to lock them out or I would be committing an unfair labour practice." This bizarre statement was true in the sense that it is an unfair labour practice in Manitoba to have non-union workers doing the work of unionized workers once a strike has come to an end, but all Engel had to do to avoid this problem was lay off the non–union workers.[20]

The only question for the union now was whether it should amend its original complaint or file a second one. Paterson and Mitic decided to hedge their bets by filing a second complaint. As Paterson put it, "That way, if we lost the first one, we had the second one to rely on. And if we won the first one we could bargain with the second one still hanging over the company's head."

The union was now seeking an additional $150,000 in lost wages and $12 million in severance. Because the charges dealt with a lockout as opposed to a strike, the labour code permitted the union to file claims against John Buhler and Craig Engel personally. This meant that the two men might find themselves on the hook financially if the Labour Board ruled against the company.

10

From Lockout to Severance

April to August 2001

The case that Garth Smorang prepared for the Labour Board essentially had two prongs. The first was to demonstrate that Buhler had engaged in behaviour that could be categorized as bargaining in bad faith. This argument involved both the content of his proposals and his attitude to the bargaining process. In preparing this portion of the case, Smorang relied heavily on notes that Dale Paterson, Scott McLaren, and Frank Tangerdy had taken throughout negotiations. As the notes described it, Buhler was not bargaining as much as throwing out ideas and concepts, constantly shifting his positions and adding to them.

These detailed notes were, Smorang said, the most important evidence in the hearing as a whole. "First of all they were dead accurate: in other words, Mr. Buhler, when he was cross-examined, was never able to say, 'I didn't say that.' And so he essentially corroborated everything that was in the notes." According to Paterson, in a normal set of negotiations he would never have taken the sort of notes generated in the Versatile talks. "It's hard being the spokesperson and writing down what you and the other person are saying. There was one meeting where we went through every item, and he said 'no' to each of them. Normally my notes would not list each one and just what management said. But this time we felt it was important to get it down in detail."

Smorang believed that the union's case would be stronger if he could provide a rationale that demonstrated why Buhler had taken an approach that had not only generated a lengthy and bitter strike, but also lost his company an important contract and led it to consider shifting operations to a foreign country. He chose to argue that all along Buhler had been more interested in getting rid of the union and moving the plant to North Dakota than he was on reaching an agreement with the CAW or making tractors in Manitoba. On the face of it, this was a stretch, but Smorang believed that the financial records leaked to the union would prove the case: because Buhler got the plant for a bargain basement price, he could afford to take chances with its future.

Since there was little chance that Buhler Versatile Industries would provide such confidential financial documents to the Labour Board or the union, Smorang had to convince the Board to compel BVI to provide the information. The Board bought his arguments, instructing Versatile to turn copies of the documentation surrounding the sale over to Smorang. Tracey Epp, the lawyer acting for Buhler Versatile, sought to severely limit the financial documentation that was presented at the Board hearing. While she believed that the financial records that the CAW and the Board were requesting were not relevant to the case, the company agreed to provide the Board with the asset purchase agreement between Buhler and CNH, the tractor supply agreement, the TV140 supply agreement, and the financial statement for the month following the purchase. Under her proposal, the documents could not be copied and they could not be made public.[1]

According to Smorang the documents allowed him and forensic accountant Allan Martyszenko "to better understand not only the terms of sale and the terms of the loan but also how he had structured things when he bought it." What they saw supported their theory: that Buhler was trying to make it as easy as he could to walk away from the government loan, to walk away from the province of Manitoba. The CAW had hired Martyszenko to review the financial documentation surrounding the case, and his testimony was to prove crucial.

Epp must have realized that the documents were going to create problems for her client. In a letter to the Board she wrote:

> it is clear that neither the CAW nor the Board has a clear understanding of why BVI took certain positions during negotiations. We anticipate that representatives of BVI will testify that most, if not all, of the positions it took were to achieve cost containment, productions [sic] flexibility and corporation growth as BVI commenced operation of its new business. Accordingly, "poverty" was NOT being pled in the traditional sense.[2]

When the Board reconvened on April 17, Epp argued that the relationship with the CAW had been poisoned by the earlier dealings between the union and Buhler at Greensteel Industries. This, not any failure to bargain in good faith, lay behind their inability to reach an early agreement. She also pointed out that the union had quietly opposed Buhler's efforts to purchase the plant. Paterson said that while the Greensteel experience had coloured the union's view of Buhler, its main reasons for opposing Buhler's purchase of the plant was his lack of an international dealer network and a marketing strategy.[3]

On April 27, Craig Engel responded in writing to the CAW's initial allegations, acknowledging that the January 15 proposal was the only written proposal provided by the company since its original September 28 proposal. But, he said, shortly after the strike started the company faxed the union a list of possible dates for negotiations and received no response. He also argued that the union had failed to respond to the offers the company tabled on September 28 and January 15. In addition, he said, the union had not responded to a company communication of October 31. He pointed out that while the company's January 15 proposals referred to the need for "discussion" of the management's ability to transfer employees, CAW proposals had also called for discussion—rather than applying formal contract language—on a number of issues. Engel reiterated his position that the lockout had been forced on the company because the union would not agree to a return-to-work agreement that would allow Versatile to bring back workers irrespective of seniority. Until there was a return-to-work agreement, Versatile would continue to use non-union labour, and because it could not use such workers unless the union was either on strike or locked out, it would have to lock the workers out. That action was, Engel wrote, temporary and "only necessary until a contract had been reached."[4]

Paterson and McLaren were the first two witnesses. Through their testimony Smorang established that Buhler had been ill-prepared, unwilling to compromise, and, in the end, bargaining backwards. When Engel and Buhler appeared as witnesses, Smorang's goal was to demonstrate why they would have placed the future of their plant in jeopardy by bargaining in bad faith. At the start of his examination of Engel, Smorang told the Board, "We believe we will show the Board that the employer was not particularly interested in running the plant as a going concern and in fact had taken interesting and drastic steps to protect himself financially should the plant shut down."

The evidence for this position came from the sales agreement information. As they read through these complex financial documents, Smorang and Martyszenko reached some surprising conclusions, demonstrating the full truth of Michael Decter's comment that Buhler was committed to "never overpay for an asset." In 2000 the news media had reported that Buhler had paid about $100 million for the plant. In discussions about the CAW's proposal that the government take over the plant, Buhler had used the figure of $90 million. In spring 2001 the CAW had publicly estimated that he paid no more than $47 million—which means that after assuming the $32-million loan, Buhler paid Case New Holland only $15 million in cash.

But it now appeared that even this price was inflated. It became apparent that during the course of negotiations Buhler and CNH came close to agreeing to a value of almost $74 million, which meant that after assuming the $32-million loan and other liabilities, Buhler would have had to pay CNH approximately $42 million. But Buhler was able to drive the price down dramatically as the deadline for the deal approached. In the end the final purchase agreement put the value of the land, buildings, and inventory at only $28 million, an amount less than the loan and other liabilities that Buhler was agreeing to take over. As a result, CNH actually agreed to *pay Buhler* the difference between the liabilities and the value of the assets: about $3.5 million. In the short term, the plant had cost Buhler nothing—he got the plant, he got a contract to build tractors for CNH, and he got $3.5 million. In the long term he was obliged to pay the government of Canada back $32 million, although the first payment would not fall due until 2003. When Engel, under examination by Smorang, revealed this information, Labour Board chairperson John Korpesho could not repress a smile. He simply commented "Not a bad deal."

The deal had other wrinkles. At the time that the loan was transferred to the newly created Buhler Versatile Industries, the company had only $100 in assets. But while BVI was responsible for repaying the loan, BVI had not taken title to the land on which the Versatile plant stood. That land, valued at $4.5 million, had been assigned to Haskett Properties, a holding company that owned the property for most of Buhler's operations. As Korpesho pointed out, "That means that if BVI shuts down, there is $4.5 million less for the federal government to look to be repaid through." BVI had also taken out two secured loans from companies related to Buhler; in the event of failure these creditors would be paid before the federal government. Reporter Martin Cash summed up the testimony:

> BVI is a wholly owned subsidiary of Buhler Industries Inc., a publicly traded company on the Toronto Stock Exchange whose majority owner is John Buhler. Although BVI owes the federal government $32 million, the government has no recourse to Buhler Industries Inc. or John Buhler or to the other subsidiary that now owns the land should BVI fall into financial difficulty.[5]

In other words, Buhler had received $3.5 million for taking over the plant, had taken over a $32-million loan—with no loan guarantees—and then arranged his finances in a way that would make it easy for him to walk away from the loan.

Another sign of the company's lack of interest in running the company as a going concern involved Engel's response to CNH's attempt to cancel the TV140 contract. Engel told the Board that he had been unaware of a ten-day grace period in the TV140 contract with CNH: the extra time would have allowed BVI to rectify the company's inability to deliver the tractor. Instead of letting the union know that a contract key to the company's future was being jeopardized by the strike, Engel took the opportunity presented by the cancellation to sell CNH $10-million worth of TV140-related inventory. His lack of knowledge of the ins and outs of a contract that he and Buhler had both described as essential to the plant's future perplexed the members of the Labour Board. Paterson told the news media at the time: "One would assume that if there's an ability to resolve something you'd think they'd come to the other party and say 'This maybe changes the whole focus of bargaining.' But they didn't do that. They elected to make the decision unilaterally without even involving the union or seeing if they could put a deal together."[6]

At the start of his testimony Buhler took the unusual step of asking to make a brief statement to the Board. With the Board's agreement he started by relating how at the age of sixteen he would "sit on the seat of a John Deere tractor and dream of someday building a tractor with the name Buhler on it." He also pointed out that his birthday was July 1, Canada Day. "I have no intention of ever leaving Canada or Manitoba. I am a proud Canadian and Manitoban and I will always live here and pay my taxes here." But, he said, the plant was doomed when the CAW rejected binding arbitration. "I realized that they were willing to jeopardize the long-term viability of the factory by causing us to lose a $100-million-dollar contract.... We were not prepared to gamble with the added uncertainty of an unstable workforce that was willing to play Russian roulette with the livelihood of so many dedicated workers— union and non-union." Once the TV140 was lost, Buhler said, he realized he had to "find workers who shared our vision of success" and that he "would have to look outside the province for that workforce."

As Smorang commented, "He sounded more like he was preaching than testifying. I don't think he realized he was in jeopardy until quite late in the process." Throughout his testimony Buhler continued to display a lack of awareness of the various protocols governing collective bargaining. At one point Labour Board member Charles McCormick felt obliged to warn Buhler that he ought to be careful in reporting what went on in the confidential mediation process with Wally Fox-Decent. During his first day of testimony Buhler told the Board, "The chances of building tractors here for the long term are gone forever." He also explained that he did business with his heart rather than his head.[7]

During Buhler's three days on the stand, Korpesho kept coming back to the TV140 deal. Why had Buhler not contacted the union when he was faced with the loss of the TV140 contract, particularly because Buhler was insisting that the loss of that contract sealed the plant's fate? Buhler's response was that at that point they were only communicating with the union through the conciliator. But, according to Paterson, the conciliator passed on to him no such message about the future of the TV140. (This may well not have been the conciliator's fault, because it does not appear that BVI asked that such a message be communicated.) There is also no provision in the mediation protocol that prohibited Buhler from contacting the union. Indeed, during this period BVI human resources officer Helen Bergen was regularly contacting the union to voice concerns over picket-line activity.[8] Under Smorang's examination Buhler acknowledged that when he bought the plant he did not know if it was profitable, if there were environmental issues associated with the plant, or the value of the severance package that the company would have to pay to the members if the plant closed.

Paul Lussier, like many striking Versatile workers, attended the Board sessions. "When I was hearing some of the things that were coming out of [Buhler's] mouth, I was just grinning from ear to ear." Once Lussier, from his seat at the back of the room, managed to catch Buhler's eye. Buhler found Lussier's grin disconcerting and complained to Korpesho about being laughed at. The Board chairperson suggested that Buhler simply look at the panel members and ignore the members of the public.

Tool-and-dye maker Joseph Smith went to the Labour Board hearings every day. "After hearing the forensic accountant and our lawyer's summary I knew we had a case." He too found himself fighting back laughter when Buhler testified. When he went back to the picket line he told everyone the union was bound to win. His confidence was based on his experience as a juror in Trinidad. "The judge told the jurors that you have to watch the accused's behaviour, his attitude, his characteristics, the way he answers questions, the reasons he gives for not telling the truth. I applied it to what I saw in the Labour Board hearing and thought the Board would find Buhler guilty."

In his testimony Martyszenko said that Buhler did not undertake the normal inquiries expected of an investor making such a significant purchase. When Korpesho asked if Buhler's due diligence, as the process of kicking the corporation's tires is called, was pretty "loosey-goosey," Martyszenko could only agree. But, he said, "In this deal Buhler minimized the risk shareholders have to take. If you minimize your risk and have the option to move you can do very well. In my opinion, due diligence was not very important." The limited degree of due diligence was, he believed, potential evidence that Buhler might well have been planning to buy the plant, close it, and transfer its operations elsewhere. Martyszenko also testified that because of how the loan was structured, its cost was actually closer to $18 million than $32 million. In response, Epp said Martyszenko was measuring Buhler's due diligence process against an idealized concept that only took place under perfect conditions. In the real world, she said, "There is no such thing as a perfect transaction. Having gone through a number of transactions myself, I know there are countless permutations and combinations and methodologies used in due diligence."[9] In other words, she did not think there was anything particularly loosey-goosey about the process.

Throughout the hearings the union and the company had been communicating through mediator Fox-Decent. On May 10 the Board, in a surprise move, recommended that both parties get back together with Fox-Decent to see if they could finally hammer out an agreement. When they met that afternoon in Smorang's office Fox-Decent gave the union a handwritten proposal from the company. The offer did not amount to a significant change, but it was a complete offer, which meant the company might be able to stop the clock on the unfair nature of the lockout. The union rejected the offer and refused to ask for an adjournment of the Labour Board hearing.[10]

On the twelfth and final day of the hearings, Epp maintained that all Buhler had done was engage in hard bargaining. "If they say you can't put an offer on the table that you know the other side will not agree to it, then what does that do to our negotiations?" It was an important question. In answering it, Smorang said, "It is the position of the Auto Workers that these losses have happened because the employer BVI didn't know or didn't care about 14 very important words in the Labour Relations Act—bargain in good faith and make every reasonable effort to conclude a collective agreement."[11] The union's argument remained that it was Buhler's intent all along to move to the United States. The evidence came from Buhler's provocative approach to bargaining, How he let the TV140 slip through his fingers, and his insistence that he get the loan without any requirement to stay in the country.

The proposition that Buhler was responsible for the strike was a high-stakes gamble. Labour boards had made similar rulings, but never in cases where so many workers had been on strike for so long. If the Board bought the CAW case, it would have little choice but to rule that the workers should be paid full wages for the time in which they had been on strike. Smorang found this prospect unsettling: "Everybody in the room knew how much money we were talking about. It made me very unsure as to whether the Board would be prepared to make that ruling understanding that it was an all or nothing proposition."

The answer came on June 7, when the Labour Board announced its initial finding: Buhler had indeed bargained in bad faith. The news was stunning.

Buhler reacted emotionally, telling CBC-Television that he was saddened to the point of tears. "I've been charged with negotiating in bad faith. Three weeks after the strike I offered binding arbitration and now I'm charged with negotiating in bad faith. I'm not that kind of a person. I'm not as bad as people say I am. But I can't undo what people choose to think."[12] He told the *Winnipeg Free Press* that he had created his last job in Manitoba. "I still plan on giving my money away, but the job-creation thing is gone forever. Why would I bother?" In what reporter Brendan O'Hallarn described as a lengthy and emotional interview, Buhler said, "The union targeted me in the community, and they successfully beat me down. Now they still want to extract money from the guy they've buried in the ground." He also blamed the NDP for the Labour Board decision: "The Manitoba (government) says if you don't give your employees everything they want, they're going to charge you with an unfair business practice. How long is a guy going to keep all his eggs in this basket when this happens?"[13]

The CAW celebrated the decision as a major victory. McLaren said, "If Mr. Buhler wants to sit down and negotiate, then we are prepared to do that. We don't think he is, but we are prepared to do that." He also renewed the union's call for the federal and provincial governments to take over the plants. As soon as the decision was released, Paterson phoned Fox-Decent to tell him that the CAW's proposed settlement offer was no longer on the table. Later that morning Fox-Decent called Paterson to let him know that he had been in conversation with Buhler, and the company was interested in further discussions.

The Local members were delirious. Smith was on the picket line listening to the radio when he heard the news. The other workers came over to him and told him, "Daddy-o, you knew what you were saying." Ray Wilkie was at the union headquarters on Grant Avenue when the news came in. "I went in to pick up my pay cheque and Scott was there. He told me that we had won. The first time I did not believe him. I said, 'Tell me again.' And he said we won. And I did not believe it. And then he told me the third time, and I hugged and kissed him. The first man I ever kissed."

The Labour Board had found for the union, but it had declined to order an award—yet. Its preference was that the two parties negotiate a settlement acceptable to both of them. On June 19 the union asked Buhler for $18 million, its estimate of the cost of the strike to March 26, the date on which the union ended the strike and the company locked the workers out. The $18 million comprised $6 million in lost wages and strike costs and $12 million in severance. And as Smorang pointed out, as long as the workers were locked out, the meter was still running, at a rate of $44,000 day.[14] Engel simply replied that the union proposal was out of line. Epp argued, "Mr. Buhler did not have the ability to put a gun to the head of the union and say 'go on strike.' The economic losses suffered by the employees were due to their own decision to go on strike."[15]

With the union and the company so far apart, the Board was forced to issue its own ruling. Not surprisingly, it ordered Buhler to cease bargaining in bad faith. It also ordered the company to withdraw its proposals that all grievances be settled prior to the agreement of the contract, as well as its proposals for overriding seniority in a return-to-work agreement. It called on the company to make a full and detailed contract offer. It ordered the company to compensate the strikers for all the wages and benefits they would have received if they had not gone out on strike. The Board left it to the company and union to agree on what this amounted to—if they could not, the Board would impose an amount.

At the time the union estimated that the wage and benefits bill for the period covered by the Labour Board ruling was between $5 million and $6 million, which would make this the largest award ever ordered by the Manitoba Labour Board. The terms and conditions of the collective agreement were to be in force until March 26, 2001. The CAW was awarded $170,000 for strike-related costs, but was not compensated for legal or expert witness fees. Finally, because the plant had not been closed down, the Board did not rule on the union's claim for $12 million in severance pay; but the Board's decision that the terms and conditions of the agreement remained in place meant that the workers would still qualify for severance pay if Buhler did close the plant.

Buhler said he felt like he had been "knocked to the floor by a power that is certainly a lot higher than anything I could ever react to, and I just don't know what's going to happen."[16] Paterson was ecstatic. "It is a day that will go down in history." To make sure the company did not try to avoid making the payment by declaring bankruptcy, the CAW filed a new application with the Labour Board that would make Buhler and Engel personally responsible for the amount.[17] McLaren and Rausch both indicated that the union was hoping to get an agreement quickly and get its members back to work. Said Rausch, "The quicker we can get back, the better it will be for all the members and their families." Buhler also announced that he might have to put the planned move to North Dakota on hold: "There won't be any money to go anywhere."[18] Engel reported that because of the strike the plant workforce would probably have to be cut by a third.[19] He also announced that the company would appeal the Labour Board decision to "the highest court in the land."[20]

From the company's point of view, the Labour Board's final ruling in the Versatile case was nothing less than devastating. The Board began by raising important questions about the management of Versatile:

> At times, it seemed unclear as to who at BVI was making the decisions on critical issues affecting the bargaining process and the survival of the plant. Buhler would have us believe that he is an unsophisticated, naïve businessman, who went into this deal with his heart because of his boyhood dream since the age of sixteen of building tractors. Yet, he allowed Engel to enter into a deal with New Holland on January 12, 2001 to cancel the TV140 contract and sell off all the inventory without informing the CAW-Canada of this critical turn of events, in order to save his dream. If Buhler or Engel had done so, the CAW-Canada would have at least been in a better position to seriously consider what options would be open to the union at that stage.

> It is also curious that, on the issue of seniority and department transfers, Engel testified that there needed to be some tinkering, while Buhler was of the view that he had to get rid of seniority entirely.[21]

Buhler's bargaining style came in for the most sustained criticism:

> There is no doubt in our minds that the CAW-Canada, from the

initial meeting of September 29th, 2000, modified and withdrew certain bargaining proposals, and at the same time asked for written clarification so they could rationally consider certain proposals put forth by Buhler. The Employer, on the other hand, offered less each time they met and failed to provide requested information in relation to its proposals.[22]

It is also our view that Buhler knew, or ought to have known, that certain of his demands that would eliminate a number of longstanding provisions in the existing Collective Agreement, including the current health and welfare benefits and seniority, could not have been accepted by the Union and still have them maintain credibility with its members.[23]

When it coupled Buhler's pattern of bargaining backwards with his behaviour at the bargaining table, the Board concluded that this was a case of bargaining in bad faith.

We are troubled that his strategy with the CAW-Canada was based on his constant threat of plant closure. Buhler's proposals seemed, at times, to be irrational, to say the least, and at certain times took on a "bait and switch" type of strategy. A number of times through the bargaining sessions Buhler insisted that he would not lock out the employees, yet in those same discussions, threatened to padlock the doors....

Buhler consistently displayed an unwillingness to enter into any rational and informed discussions and provide supporting argument throughout those negotiations. The evidence is clear that each time the CAW-Canada modified its position, Buhler proceeded to offer less. This, in itself, satisfies the Board that he breached the duty to bargain in good faith by purposely avoiding attempts to find some "common ground" to resolving outstanding issues....

Buhler's tactics can only be described as an attempt to bully the CAW-Canada into submission, by threats of selling the operation or padlocking the doors. Buhler and Engel were also quick to place the blame of the failed negotiations on the failure of both the Conciliation Officer and the Mediator for either not transmitting information or not holding face-to-face meetings with the parties. We find these comments unacceptable and consistent with Buhler's attitude that everyone else is responsible for the present situation except Buhler.

There is no doubt, in analyzing this situation, that BVI placed the CAW-Canada in a situation where negotiations were going nowhere and, in fact, in a situation where each time they met, the Employer's offer worsened. Buhler's proposals could best be described as a "moving target."[24]

The Board concluded that the "Employer's conduct during the bargaining sessions, up to and including November 2nd, 2000, were such that they contravened the duty to bargain in good faith and to make every reasonable effort to enter into a collective agreement."[25] The failure to inform the union about the potential loss of the TV140 constituted a second breach of the act.

Local 2224 had taken an all-or-nothing proposition to the Labour Board, pressing a charge that was extraordinarily difficult to prove. It had won a clear-cut victory, one virtually without precedent. While Smorang was largely responsible for the legal victory, it was the membership's unity and determination that had brought the case before the Labour Board in the first place. Given the national union's apprehension about the cost and risks of even levelling charges of bad-faith bargaining, the Local would not have been able to pursue the charges if there had been dissension in the union or a falling away of support for the strike.

The *Free Press* editorial board put an unusual spin on the story, arguing that the workers at Versatile had simply been pawns in a larger game:

> The Versatile plant was a bit of industrial flotsam left over from a U.S. corporate merger, an orphan plant that nobody wanted. John Buhler was paid to take ownership to solve a problem for the New Holland Corporation. Versatile's prospects of survival were not good. For the Canadian Auto Workers, it seemed important for bargaining elsewhere that no concessions or give-backs should be granted to the employer. The doomed Versatile plant and its few jobs were relatively expendable. In these conditions, there was little reason to hope that the company and the union would agree and every reason to expect a strike or a lockout.[26]

The editorial's a-plague-on-both-your-houses approach conveniently overlooked how the members of Local 2224 did not go on strike at the bidding of their national leadership—indeed, Paterson had argued for a more cautious approach. The decision not to make the sorts of concessions Buhler was asking for was not dictated by the union but by the members, who were anything but pawns in this conflict.

The union had won, but one major concern remained—would it ever be able to collect from Buhler? The information revealed during the Labour Board hearings had not been encouraging on this point. McLaren said, "All our members knew that this was a $100 company. If we sued for our money, we might get nothing." Smorang worried that the company might move to the United States immediately:

> There might be a movement of assets. If there was, then that might leave us unable to collect on our award. It was clear from the way the company had structured itself and divested itself of important assets like land and buildings, that if we got an award against Buhler Versatile itself, we may not be able to collect anything.

Still, the union was holding a high card—its second unfair labour practice charge. According to Smorang, "It was absolutely clear that we were going to win that one." That second charge seemed likely to lead to another large award. That possibility, according to Smorang, placed even more pressure on Buhler to come to an agreement and get the workers back into the plant—because for every day that went by without an agreement the owner was going to have to pay "something like $40,000 a day."

While many of the union members had long despaired of ever returning to work at Versatile, the Labour Board victory had renewed their hopes. Buhler had been ordered to bargain with them and to withdraw some of his most objectionable proposals. There was now reason to think that the union and Buhler could reach an agreement that would see at least some of them returning to work. With this in mind the union made contact with Engel in hopes of reopening negotiations. The union's strategy was to reach an agreement on a return-to-work protocol that would see the lockout ended. After that, the union and company could return to bargaining.

The first meeting was set for Friday, July 27. As head of the bargaining committee, McLaren was hoping that it might be possible to reach an agreement that would finally end the conflict.

> We thought he was going to come to the table and sit down and negotiate a contract. We thought we were going to get the six

million dollars, or at least we were hoping that. But our major goal was to get people back to work. The business was suffering, our jobs were in jeopardy. We were hoping he would offer us a complete status quo. Money would be good, but people really wanted to go back to work.

On Friday morning Engel showed up at the CAW offices with two senior Winnipeg lawyers, Doug Ward and Paul Walsh. Paterson took this as a good sign. "I thought we were going to get into heavy-duty bargaining and negotiate an agreement, get fifty people to work right away." The bargaining session was only a few minutes old when Ward asked for a private meeting with Hemi Mitic. He and Engel presented Mitic with a unique proposal: BVI was prepared to make a $16-million payment. In exchange for this money the workers would have to sever their relationship with the company, and the union would drop its second Labour Board charge. The strike would be over, but to get their pay all the union members would have to quit. Engel also indicated that the company still intended to close the Winnipeg plant. Mitic was taken completely by surprise by the proposal. He said the only way to find out how the bargaining team would take such a proposal would be to put it on the table.

They returned to the larger group and placed the proposal before the bargaining committee. McLaren recalled, "We were taken aback. It was not what we were expecting at all. We said we would entertain the idea, but could not say more than that." It was undoubtedly the first offer from Buhler Versatile that the union could consider seriously. Lussier was stunned by the proposal. "Nobody saw it coming. Nobody." Paterson later commented that it was as out of left field as the CAW's proposal to end the strike in March. He thought, "Buhler has finally come to terms with the nature of the problem he is in. He has asked the right question, how do I get out of this and has been told, there is only one way, you are going to have to pay."

The offer had two important elements: it was comprehensive, in that it dealt with all the union's financial issues, and it represented a guaranteed payment. To Smorang, "This was not only a way to wrap it up entirely but also to guarantee the workers that they would actually get a cheque." Still, the offer was not an easy one for the bargaining committee members to accept. Personally, McLaren was reluctant to agree to the proposal.

I thought that our second case at the Labour Board was strong. We were going to win another big award, more than Buhler was offering. But I also knew that if we went that route there was no guarantee of payment. And he is still talking about shutting down the plant and moving it to the U.S. So even if we get a contract more than half the people on strike are never going back to work at Versatile, not even in the short term. And we also had a responsibility not only to the 250 people on strike, but the 250 people on layoff. This deal would give everyone some sort of severance package.

Bargaining team member Winston Johnson thought the deal made it look as if the workers were simply interested in the money, not their jobs. But, like McLaren, he eventually came around to supporting the agreement. He feared that if the union turned the offer down, Buhler might declare bankruptcy. "We had to consider that for our membership." During the lengthy strike the number of people eligible for recall had fallen from close to 450 to 250. If the strike had continued, even more people would have lost their rights to recall and severance.

Once the team decided to accept the idea of a comprehensive package, it had to decide if $16 million was enough. After all, at one point the union had been asking for $18 million as compensation for the first unfair labour practice charge. If it was unable to win the second charge—and that seemed certain—it might well have a claim for $6 million in wages from the first case, $6 million in wages from the second case, and $12 million in severance. Potentially Buhler would be on the hook for $24 million, not $16 million.

The union's claim to $12 million in severance was not airtight. While the Labour Board had ruled that the severance provision was in effect if Buhler closed the plant, neither Buhler nor the CAW was calling this a plant closure. Also, the wording of the severance article was ambiguous: from the union's reading of the article, it appeared that the workers were owed about $12 million, but an arbitrator could conclude that it was worth closer to $6 million. If the union rejected the deal there was no guarantee that the company would agree to include such a generous severance package—or any severance package— in a new collective agreement. In other words, to hold out for the full $12 million in severance pay could risk losing it all. Then too, while the union's second Labour Board case was strong, the outcome was not guaranteed. Even if it won the second case, Buhler might either appeal both Labour Board decisions in the courts, delaying any payment for years, or simply declare bankruptcy. It had taken years of courtroom battle before the union members collected the money the Labour Board awarded them in 1985. By going for the $24-million victory, the union might end up with nothing. It was too big a risk to take. The bargaining committee attempted to increase the size of the payout, but in typical Buhler style it was made clear that the first offer was going to be the best offer. It was, as McLaren put it, too big an offer not to take back to the members.

After the bargaining team decided that it was going to recommend the proposal to the membership it had to determine how the money was to be divided. On this, the union took a two-step approach. The first step was to implement the Labour Board award, which provided the strikers with their full pay for the time spent out on strike, which was until the lockout at the end of March. After deducting strike pay and any income the members had earned from other jobs taken during the course of the strike, the union would pay workers a total of $3.9 million to compensate them for lost wages until March 26.

While this first payment was straightforward, the second step, which came to be termed the retirement allowance, was more complicated. Because there was no plant closure, Buhler was not making a payment based on the severance provisions of the collective agreement. The bargaining team members had to decide who would be covered and how the money was to be distributed. While the union could have restricted this payment to the members who had been out on strike, the leadership decided that it ought to be divided between both the strikers and those on layoff. McLaren said, "Legally we could have kept it to the strikers, but we felt we had a moral obligation to all our members." The leaders devised a formula ensuring that those who had been locked out from the end of March to August 13 did not lose income after the strike. After strike pay and outside earnings were deducted, another $3.9 million would be paid to the strikers. The remaining $5.9 million would be divided among the five hundred or so members who had been eligible for severance pay.

The union had a number of estimates of the impact of the deal on various workers. A material hander with twenty-five years of seniority could expect $33,000 in wages and $15,000 in retirement allowance. A skilled tradesman with computer skills and twenty-seven years' seniority could expect $40,000 in wages and $19,000 in retirement allowance. The CAW would receive $2.3 million as compensation for the strike pay that had gone to the workers and a number of its strike-related costs as ordered by the Labour Board. The CAW's decision to recoup its strike pay was to prove one of the most controversial elements of the agreement.

In addition to the financial settlement, both parties agreed to end the various civil actions and injunctions initiated during the strike. Furthermore, the CAW agreed to withdraw its actions before the Labour Board and give up its right to represent Versatile workers. If future Versatile workers were to approach the CAW, the union would have the right to organize them and once more seek certification from the Labour Board. Finally Buhler had to make a commitment to meet any unfunded pension obligations—which in the end amounted to $1.5 million. In other words, the total amount Buhler had to pay to make the union go away was $17.5 million: the $16 million settlement plus the $1.5 million payment to the pension plan. Buhler would not have been required to make that payment if the union had not successfully lobbied for changes to the pension regulations the year before.

This, then, was the final offer. The big question was, would the members buy it?

As union members filed into a meeting room at the Fairmont Hotel on August 13, the union and the company were still working out the final details of the agreement. At the last minute the company was demanding a provision prohibiting the strikers from applying anew for jobs at the company. "We were having none of it," McLaren said. His position was, "If Buhler does not want them to work there, he can tell them." The demand was a potential breaker. "A lot of us would continue fighting on, we would be happy to have a reason to walk away from the deal." While Smorang arranged to have copies of the agreement made, the bargaining team members rushed to the hotel and began to summarize what for many members was a shocking proposal. It was not an easy meeting for McLaren. He had to tell people, "If you vote for this you are out of a job. You are never going back to Versatile. You are going to get your wages, your retirement allowance, and not much more. And we are recommending it."

Picket captain Richard Ullmann opposed the agreement. "I didn't think I would be able to go back to work, but I was hoping that a number of people in production would be able to go back to work. I think we should have stuck it out and really got a victory. Basically Buhler won, I think. He had to pay out some money but then again he got the plant for next to nothing." Others, like Mel Resler, were ready to move on. "I thought that the agreement was good." He thought he would at least be able to get on with his life and get a job elsewhere.

Smorang found the meeting a sobering event. "There were several hundred guys who were all going to lose their jobs. It's all well and good to say to somebody 'Here's a cheque for $40,000,' but if that's the last

cheque you see in your working career, then $40,000 isn't a lot at all."
Despite some obvious unhappiness, Smorang was impressed that there
was no recrimination at the meeting. "I don't recall anyone jumping up
and accusing the leaders of selling them out." He attributed that mood to
two factors: strong leadership and the structure of the bargaining committee and executive.

> We had fourteen guys around the table at any given time, and
> every one of those had an equal say. Every one of those fourteen
> had to understand what was going on and had to agree with what
> was going on, and quite deliberately these guys represented
> different factions both departmentally, also on ethnic basis, these
> people were picked to represent constituencies. Everybody knew
> that this was the moment of truth. There wasn't any divisiveness,
> certainly nothing like I might have expected.

There were also many unanswered questions. The workers were
leaving without knowing what was going to happen to the plant. Was
Buhler going to keep it open and have other people run it? Was he going
to move to the States? Others wanted to know who was actually going
to be paying them—many suspected it was New Holland that was
stepping in to shut Buhler up and shut down their plant. In the end the
strikers accepted the deal by a vote of 177 to 13. As they left the hotel the
members told the news media that they were glad to be getting a
payment but upset about losing their jobs. A muted Paterson described it
as "the best of a bad situation."[27]

For most of the strikers, the hardest part of the deal to swallow was
the union's decision on strike pay: the CAW was going to get $2.3
million to cover the strike pay that members had received during the
strike. Louis Mora calls this the only black mark on the union's behaviour during the strike. "I did not think it was right then and I do not
think it is right now. If we were going back to work, I would say, 'Ok,
we were going back to work. The money should have gone to the
people who were on the picket line.'" Sandy Brar also opposed the
national union's decision to recoup its strike pay. As he recalled, he told
Mitic, "This is the workers' money. You can take that money if we can
settle with this person and the whole membership [goes] back to work."
Beyond that point, however, Brar had nothing but praise for the CAW.
"The union did really a fantastic job for us. When I sent a bill they never
questioned me. That's why I was personally a little disappointed. For the
union $2 million is nothing."

From the CAW's perspective, strike pay goes to workers who are on strike, in lieu of the company's payment. Since Versatile was now paying the workers for the time that they spent on strike, the union had a right to reclaim the strike fund money. The union had a responsibility to all of the other CAW members who had contributed to the fund and might one day need to draw on it to maintain the fund's integrity. While many of the Versatile workers recognized the logic of this argument, they still resented the union decision. McLaren said that while he could see both sides of the issue, he wished the union had seen its way not to take this money.

Like many family members, Sherry Ullmann was taken aback by the agreement. "No matter how bad it got, there is always that hope that things will turn around. Buhler would back off from his demands or someone else would step in and say this was wrong." She was shocked by the idea that her husband would no longer work for Versatile. "We were at the age where it is very hard to make a career change."

Reporter Martin Cash expressed surprise that the company had agreed to provide the workers with any financial compensation at all. Engel told him, "We have things we want to do, they have things they want to do. This is a full and final release. It leaves the possibility for a positive future for both of us. They can go away and do what it is they are going to do and we'll carry on and make tractors." Tracey Epp told Cash, "John [Buhler] does not want to spend the next five years in litigation. No matter who won or lost there would be an appeal. The first hearings were extremely hard on him. The negative publicity, although he also had a quite a bit of support, was bothersome to him. With further litigation that would continue."[28]

Once the agreement was approved, a seemingly endless set of hurdles had to be crossed before money could be paid out. While the workers were to get their full wages for the period of the strike, those workers who had quit, retired, or died during the strike would only receive compensation until the date they severed their relationship with the company. Nor could anyone who had ended their relationship with the company prior to August 13, 2001, receive a severance payment. McLaren, Letwyn, and Lussier had to ensure that over five hundred people signed releases. According to Letwyn, "We had to call and call and call. A lot of people had problems. They had personal problems, they'd bring them in. Sometimes I would sit in with Scotty to talk to them, try to help them out." The union held mass information sessions, but many people had to be visited individually and have the details of the agreement explained to them before they signed. Smorang would then send a copy of the release to the firm handling the case for Buhler.

Smorang spent hours with company lawyer Michael Hicks, poring over lists, double-checking numbers, and cross-checking cheques. At the end of each of the sessions he would walk back to his office with three to four million dollars' worth of cheques in his briefcase. With the Local officers working quickly, every cheque was available by the end of the year.

Even though the union had recovered the wages that workers had lost during the strike and a substantial portion of their severance pay, many union members faced a bleak future. None of the strikers had less than twenty years' seniority. Many were in their late forties or early fifties. Many were highly skilled industrial workers, but the demand for their skills were soft. Shortly after the Versatile strike Motor Coach Industries, a Manitoba bus-manufacturing firm, threatened to close its Winnipeg plant and move to North Dakota. While the plant did stay in Manitoba, the company ended up laying off many of its workers. The New Flyer bus company was also hit by a market downturn. Tool-and-dye makers, machinists, and welders, no matter how skilled they were, could not count on finding jobs quickly and easily.

Many of the workers had come to Versatile fresh out of high school. The skills and training they developed with Versatile were at times company-specific and lacking in any sort of certification. Local 2224 had always played an important role in helping people with workers' compensation, employment insurance, and upgrading. That role continued past the shutdown as McLaren and Rausch organized a major worker adjustment program. The union approached Buhler Versatile for funding for the program, but the company was not prepared to participate. Instead the Manitoba government agreed to pay the full cost of the adjustment process. A workforce adjustment centre operated out of the CAW office for ten months, with the union providing use of offices, boardrooms, computers, printers, and resources from its national office. The workers were offered assistance in blueprint reading, welding, forklift certification, English as a second language, and high-school upgrading. Nearly two hundred workers registered with the centre. Of those, 159 participated in employment counselling, 152 completed resumés, 27 completed high-school upgrading and computer courses, and 86 completed forklift and blueprint training.

During these long months Local 2224 was there providing assistance to its members. But by June 2002 the end had come. It had been nearly two years since any of the Local members had worked at Versatile, nearly a year since the end of the strike. While the bitterness that the men harboured towards John Buhler would never disappear, most of them were moving on with their lives.

11

Between the Devil
and the Deep Blue Sea

From January 15, 2001, to August 13, 2001, John Buhler steadfastly maintained that union intransigence was forcing him to close the Buhler Versatile plant and move it to North Dakota. He told Canadian Auto Workers national president Buzz Hargrove that there was no point in the two of them trying to work out an agreement because the plant had no future. It was a position he reiterated in interview after interview. Without the TV140 contract, the plant was doomed. When the Local 2224 bargaining team recommended to the members that they had best accept Buhler's offer to buy them out, they did so on the understanding that there would be no jobs to return to because Buhler intended to close the plant.

In announcing the agreement between the CAW and Buhler Versatile, Craig Engel explained that the payout would not have a negative impact on the Buhler empire: "Reserves had been set up during the year to partially cover this outcome. The potential sale of some intellectual property will cover the balance. A cash infusion by John Buhler personally will assist in funding this settlement."[1] Buhler told *The Globe and Mail* that he had mortgaged his house to finance the deal. In an interview with the *Free Press* he said he had been forced to mortgage everything he owned, and then he added the kicker. As a result of the settlement, he said, "There's no money for Fargo."[2] Just days after his lawyers told the workers the plant was closing, he was now telling the news media that the plant was going to stay put in Winnipeg. To many CAW members, this was Buhler's final betrayal.

Not only did Buhler keep the Winnipeg plant open, but Case New Holland also extended his contract, which would allow him to continue building tractors for them until summer 2002. It turns out that the TV140 contract was nowhere near as important to the plant's future as Buhler had maintained. In summer 2002 Buhler did buy a former John Deere factory in Fargo, but he used it to build loaders, mowing equipment, and some components for the tractor operation.

After the strike ended, Engel declined to reveal how many people were working at the Versatile plant or how many tractors the plant was producing.[3] The dealer network remained small; by spring 2003 Engel could lay claim to only 170 dealers.[4] He said that the company was picking up twenty-five new dealers every three months, but by the end of 2003 the company still had only 200 dealers.[5] In contrast, Case New Holland had 12,000 dealers in 160 countries. Buhler was making far fewer appearances in the press than he had in the past, but in the summer of 2003 he told a reporter in Regina that the Versatile strike had been caused by the union's demand for "huge increases" that he could not afford to pay.[6] Even during the strike he had acknowledged that the issues were benefits and seniority, not wages. As for the famous federal government loan, according to Engel the company intended to start paying it back in fall 2003.[7]

Today, although Buhler Industries remains a very profitable operation, the Buhler line of tractors does not represent a serious threat to CNH or John Deere. Nor is it clear how Buhler will be able to upgrade his product lines in the future. New Holland thought nothing of spending $40 million and two years to develop a new Genesis tractor. It is doubtful whether Buhler Versatile has the engineering talent and capital to make such a commitment to product development, particularly since its dealer network is comparatively small.

Former Local 2224 president Len Rausch has an anecdote that underlines the dangers of being owned by a multinational corporation. During a meeting with company president Paul Soubry in the 1990s, when the plant was owned by Fiat, Rausch asked Soubry if he thought Fiat president Giovanni Agnelli even knew about the Versatile plant in Winnipeg. When Soubry replied that he was certain Agnelli knew about the Winnipeg operation, a dubious Rausch said, "He owns hundreds of companies around the world and he knows we're here? Paul, name me thirty of your closest relatives, right now." According to Rausch, Soubry was able to name twenty-five or twenty-six relatives, but could not reach thirty.

Global manufacturing corporations are more likely to be prepared to deal with unions, and to pay good wages and benefits (in large measure because their global reach and protection from competition allow them to pass these costs on to consumers). Certainly, for Local 2224 members the Ford and Fiat years were better than their brief but bitter experience with Buhler. But when you fall off the multinational radar screen, the drop can be sudden and precipitous.

The Versatile workers were not the only agricultural implement workers who saw the bottom fall out of their world in 2000. In July 2000, when the U.S. Justice Department gave its final blessing to the merger of Case and New Holland, CNH executives announced that they would be closing twenty-one of sixty existing plants by the end of 2005. This, they predicted, would result in a profit improvement of $433 million by 2003. Not surprisingly, they were silent about the amount of suffering that the lost jobs would create around the world.

As it closed plants CNH continued to market both Case and New Holland tractors brands, but from 2002 onwards CNH began building both lines of tractors on the same assembly line, in Mount Pleasant, Illinois. Mark Koznarek, an analyst with Midwest Research of Cleveland, said that this common assembly line, which was expected to save the company $280 million by 2005, was "really the whole reason for the merger." The common assembly line was also expected to lead to the elimination of an undetermined number of UAW jobs in the Racine area. Those jobs losses were compounded by CNH's decision to close its Racine foundry in May 2004, putting one hundred employees out of work.[8]

Despite these moves, the newly created company not only lost market share to John Deere, but also lost $381 million in 2000 and $332 million in 2001. After losing 4.3 billion Euros in 2003 Fiat announced it would be closing twelve more plants around the world, laying off 12,300 workers in the process. Five CNH factories, with 4,000 workers, were on the list of operations slated to be shut down. Because Italian unions had responded to a round of layoffs with demonstrations and plant occupations in 2002, Fiat management announced that this time most of the job losses would take place outside of Italy.[9]

Nor was AGCO, another potential purchaser of Versatile, faring much better. In 2003 it reported decreased sales and earnings; it closed its British plant and moved production to Brazil.[10] While John Deere continued to dominate the industry, its success was built in part on its ability to downsize and to wring concessions from the workers that remained. In 1994 Deere had 11,000 U.S. workers; by 2003 the number was down to 7,000. In 1997 it forced its workers to adopt a two-tier wage system, which meant that newly hired workers would never reach the same salary levels as long-term employees.[11]

In short, the past decade had been a bad time to be a tractor factory worker. The best that a U.S. tractor worker could hope for would be a six-year contract with only a mild reduction in benefits. Many workers lost their jobs when their plants were closed. As the Versatile story demonstrates, local capitalists were likely to make the gutting of the union contract part of the price paid by union members just to keep their jobs.

For many Local 2224 members the Versatile strike was nothing less than a disaster. Several people declined to be interviewed for this book for just that reason. One man said the strike had messed up his life, and he wanted never to speak of it again. Another, one of the founders of the Local, could barely contain his anger at New Holland, at Buhler, and at the CAW. Among his losses he listed his marriage, his family, his home, and his livelihood. He was on layoff at the start of the strike and angry because he had not been allowed to participate in the strike vote or the vote on the final package. Several people spoke of one troubled man, on layoff during the strike, who committed suicide after Buhler threatened to close the plant. Suicides never have a single cause, but many of the strikers believed that the proposed shutdown had robbed this man of hope for the future.

Few of the Versatile employees had been on the job market in twenty years. For many English was their second language. Others had never had any training other than their on-the-job experience at Versatile. In Stan Letwyn's opinion, "John Buhler and New Holland ruined a lot of lives, caused a lot of people to retire early." Some of his co-workers, he said, would have been embarrassed to take a job working with a guy, twenty years younger, giving them orders. "We were at an age when the people should have been taking it easy now. They had ten years left to go or five years left to go to retirement."

Bill Sokoliuk now works as a porter in the St. Boniface General Hospital. It is, as he acknowledged a tough job. As he said, "I had a good job once. I made $20 an hour and I had respect for the wage. We worked—and if one of your co-workers was not working you told him to pick up the slack." He would, he said, have been content to work at Versatile until he retired. Instead he was still picking up the pieces. For months after the strike ended, Sokoliuk was embarrassed about having lost his job. "I couldn't talk to anybody about it. I worked so many years and then all of a sudden I'm out the door. I was embarrassed for that. I mean, I didn't commit a crime." What he found frustrating was the idea held by so many people that the union was striking for more pay. "I was so sick and tired of explaining to everybody. I figured I would just sit in the house."

After twenty-five years with the company, electrician Ray Wilkie had been thinking about retirement. "I really had to pull myself together. At first I did not want to work again, I just felt so let down by the company and the government. I would just be a bum and collect some money from government." His son and his brother-in-law had also worked at Versatile, so the strike and the final job loss hit the family hard. Today he is working in a kitchen cabinet factory and no longer as an electrician.

Even though he is a skilled machinist, Winston Johnson has had trouble finding work in his field. "There are plenty of machinists out there, including plenty from Versatile." In 2003 he was employed at the Winnipeg Regional Health Authority with hopes of working his way into the maintenance department. With the jobs there protected by seniority, he continued to wait for an opening and an opportunity.

Tractor mechanic Dwight Pitcher said it took years for him to reach the point of being prepared to talk about the strike. "The biggest thing about this strike is that we had to change the way we live our life. I went from making fifty grand a year to making twenty-five. That is a radical change. It affects how we feed our kids, how we clothe our kids, how we educate our kids. It affects every aspect of our lives." He now works for Pauwels Canada in a unionized job, but he has lost the twenty-one years of seniority built up at Versatile. In the middle of his life, he is starting at the bottom of the seniority ladder.

The strike exacted a terrible toll from these men: the losses have been financial, psychological, and emotional. Given this great price, the question remains: did the workers make a terrible mistake by going on strike in the fall of 2000? Would it have been better to accept the cuts and live to fight another day?

The answer to this question, surprisingly, is probably not. It is pointless to speculate on Buhler's original intentions for the plant—he may have intended from the outset to move to North Dakota, or that may have simply been a bluff. He may have had a passion for making tractors, or that could have been just so much malarkey. What is certain is that he has a passion for making money. It is also equally clear that he did not have the financial resources to compete internationally with John Deere and Case New Holland. But if he could get the plant at a low enough price, if he could get the federal loan, if he could get his suppliers to cut costs, and if he could reduce the size of his workforce and their wages and benefits, he might be able to carve out a small profitable niche in the tractor market. He might not be able to occupy that niche forever, but since he did not have to put up any of his own money the risks would be small. "Buhler logic" being what it is, it is hard to tell what his original intentions were, except that he was clearly determined to rip the heart out of the CAW contract.

The negotiations of 2000 presented Local 2224 members with a dilemma. If they had accepted Buhler's conditions—which in the early stages of bargaining were never spelled out in detail—some of the workers might have kept their jobs. The price would be huge cuts in benefits, the end of seniority, and the elimination of their severance plan. If the union had moved in that direction, at least 150 workers would have been laid off, and as time passed they too would have lost their right to be recalled. With the sorts of changes in seniority that Buhler was seeking, the corporate goal was clearly a workplace in which management handpicked the employees that stayed and the ones that were laid off. No matter which road the workers chose to travel down, most of them would have lost their jobs, while the rest would have seen their benefits slashed and their job security undermined. Their only choice was whether they would walk this road individually or whether they would stick to the union.

The commitment that most of these men had to the union did not come from ideology, but from experience. They had been there in the days of the Association, when the wages were low, benefits minimal, and the foreman was all powerful. The sense of humiliation that people experienced at the prospect of having to pay a bribe, even a bottle of whiskey, to get a good shift was still fresh, as were memories of seeing older workers laid off while the foreman's friends were protected. The decision to join a real union had not been easy. People had lost their jobs during the unsuccessful campaign of the early 1980s, while the lockout of 1985 made it clear that the company was prepared to risk everything to keep the union out. The CAW had stuck by the workers through two drives, and the workers found that by sticking together they had been able to make real gains.

In the world of industrial workers in Manitoba, the Local 2224 wages and benefits were excellent; and the contract allowed them to stand up to the petty tyranny of the foreman. When a foreman gave union committeeman Louis Mora the brush-off, explaining that he did not have the time to discuss an unresolved issue, Mora and his co-workers decided not to put in any more overtime. Mora told the foreman, "If you do not have time to talk to us, we don't have time to get this job done." The foreman made the time, and the issue was resolved. Through the union the workers were able to establish that they were human beings first of all, not simple factors of production—and had to be taken into account as such. To them the union was something that they had created through their own sacrifice and solidarity. In the end they went on strike and held together because Buhler refused to treat them and their union with respect. That is why most of the workers had few regrets about their decision to go on strike.

In the summer of 2001, Ed Balik's working career came to a sudden, and in his opinion, early finish. He was sixty-three years old. "Who would hire me, what would they pay? Seven or eight dollars an hour?" He was a proud, talented man who would have loved to have continued working at Versatile making tractors. But Balik felt Buhler's approach to seniority had left him with little choice but to go on strike. "He would kick us out one by one. No consideration if you worked twenty-five years, if you worked fifty years, he doesn't like you—out, out, out, out." Speaking about the strike saddened him, but he had no regrets. For such a quiet and thoughtful man, the depth of his feelings about Buhler is surprising. As he walked me out of his house on a beautiful spring morning he said, "You know, they say that Leonardo da Vinci searched through all the prisons of Milan to find a face for Judas to use in *The Last Supper*. Today, all he would have to do is look at Buhler."

Bill Sokoliuk could not find the words to express his feelings about Buhler. While he regretted the outcome of the strike, he did not regret the steps the union had taken. "He didn't break up this union. We could have lost everything but we stuck together." Ray Wilkie echoed this sentiment:

> The longer the strike went on, the more I got to know about Mr. Buhler, the more I realized that he would have kicked us out anyway. The union did everything possible to settle this strike. The government did everything possible. He refused. So how could I regret my decision? He would kick us right out. I would have lost my job and I would not get nothing, nothing.

Later on, Wilkie added, "God bless the CAW. I wouldn't hesitate to recommend them. These guys saved a lot of people."

Winston Johnson's only regret was that he had lost a very good job. Johnson said that he thought the members hung together for so long because they were committed to the union bargaining position. The membership demands, he said, weren't pulled out of a hat, they were decided on at a duly constituted union meeting that listed priorities and determined what the members were not prepared to give up. "The membership hung in there because they believed in the union, they believed in the cause, they knew the union brought them great benefits and they were prepared to see it to the end, which they did."

Former bargaining team member Mel Resler is now working as a millwright, but he will never be able to gain the seniority he earned in twenty-seven years at Versatile. Many of the people he worked with at Versatile have seen their wages cut in half, but none of the ones he has kept in touch with have any regrets. "It was about respect. We needed his respect, because without that respect you cannot respect your employer or yourself."

To Stan Letwyn it seemed as if the bottom fell out of the industrial labour market just as the strike ended. "None of the big companies, Bristol, Standard Aero, Boeing, are hiring. People are not hiring in the industry that we worked in." The people who suffered the most from the strike, he said, are the "people who stuck with the union right to the end and the people who stayed on the picket line" because the jobs were gone when they finally went looking for work. "I'll never make what I made at Versatile." Despite all this, Letwyn said the union had no alternative but to strike:

> The alternative was that in six months or a year we had fifty people working there, everybody else would be gone, and we wouldn't have a dime in our pocket. At least this way we went out with a little bit of pride and dignity. We held our integrity and we showed Manitoba business and the people what John Buhler was all about.

Scott McLaren, now working for the CAW, looked back on the events with a mixture of pride and wonder. "This is an important event in Manitoba labour history, one people will look back on fifty years from now. We all took some terrible losses. But I feel that I came through this as a stronger person than I was before—there is not much that I would be afraid to take on now." Like Letwyn, McLaren believed that by sticking together the workers would able to achieve the very best result from the very bad hand they had been dealt.

> *"Before the plant was sold, Gary Doer stood right there in my foyer, and said, 'we are going to back you Versatile guys.' But when push came to shove after they were elected, they did not want to interfere with business."*
> —Cathy Pitcher, wife of Versatile tractor mechanic Dwight Pitcher.

Some two years after the strike ended, many Local 2224 members were still bitter about the NDP government's behaviour. Lussier recalled, "Gary Doer was at one of our rallies and swore up and down that he would take care of that plant, that it was staying here, the jobs were staying here, he'd do everything he could to make sure that happened, which he didn't. I think we were sold out by the guy." Lussier thought that the federal and provincial governments ought to have taken over the plant to protect its investment. "They could have got the same sweet deal as Buhler, taken the plant over for nothing and protected their loan. They could have made tractors for CNH for two years. We would have had our jobs for two years and if nothing else came up in the meantime they could have closed the plant."

Balik, who came to Canada thirty years earlier to escape Soviet-style communism, was puzzled by how the provincial and federal governments were prepared to let the plant slip away. "This company, its product, was famous around the world. Saudi Arabia, Australia, you name it, the tractors were going everywhere and competing with huge companies like John Deere. And the Canadian government could not do anything to stop this?" For Letwyn, as for so many others, the strike left many unanswered questions. Was Buhler merely running the plant into the ground at New Holland's request? Were any other companies offered the same sweet deal that New Holland provided to Buhler? And why hadn't the NDP done more—if not buy the plant, at least bring in anti-scab legislation and arbitrate an end to the dispute? "I am mad at Doer, he is the one who wouldn't bring it in." At the same time Letwyn was grateful to Barrett for the amendments she had made to provincial pension regulations. "She deserves big kudos in my book. Me and Scott McLaren met with her and we gave her a goodbye watch when she retired from politics."

On August 23, 2001, just ten days after the Versatile strike ended, Premier Doer stepped into the lion's den, addressing the CAW national conference in Quebec City. In introducing Doer to the delegates, Buzz Hargrove reminded them that the union had been "mad as hell at him for a while during the Versatile dispute, but in spite of that, he had the courage to be with us today." When it came his turn to speak, Doer referred to how unhappy he had been about how the Versatile strike had played out. He told the delegates, "I remain committed, when we're talking about Versatile or any other plant in Manitoba, to try and find a solution with your union, with your workers. And I regret that we weren't able to do that with Versatile." He concluded by saying that workers wanted straight talk. "They want us to admit when we made a mistake. They want us to admit when we failed to get results. We failed to get results at Versatile. We failed." But what was the failure that Doer was speaking of? When I asked him about the speech in spring 2004, Doer said, "The word 'we' was used in the speech. I think we all failed. I think the union failed, I think the employer failed, I think the government failed. Where did the government fail? We failed to get the parties together before they bargained. In November, we failed to impress upon people that the situation was serious and they should go to arbitration." Doer stood behind his government's decision not to buy the plant. Provincial government officials had concluded that the threatened move to Fargo was a bargaining ploy. Given the low Canadian dollar, the Fargo labour market, and the relatively small amount of land that Buhler owned in Fargo, Doer said, "I did not believe they were going to go south." Nor was he keen on buying a plant in the middle of a labour dispute:

> We could not have taken the plant over on the basis of a strike. If a dispute hits the rocks, you have to have incentives for both sides to come to a settlement. The worst time to walk into a takeover is on the basis of a labour management dispute. We cannot go around nationalizing every company when there is a dispute that does not go the right way.

Doer was sensitive to charges of having let the workers down, and accepted that the workers remained bitter. "We knew people who were on strike. We all felt horrible the way it went." Still, he said, "The worst thing you can do is create a false hope. That is why I made our position clear from the outset." Doer maintained that the government also could "not do the bargaining for somebody else." The government could not be "a surrogate representative for both the owner and the workers. In collective bargaining there are two equals that try to find an agreement. I regret that we did not find an agreement." He insisted that he had lived up to his early 2000 commitment to move heaven and earth to help find a purchaser for the plant.

Rausch and McLaren were philosophical about the NDP decision not to buy the plant. Despite their unhappiness about the government's inability to intervene effectively during the strike, both men continued to support the NDP in the spring 2003 provincial election. Rausch commented, "You can't have everything. Something happens, you move on. It's like if your garden freezes, well you don't sit down and say you're never going to plant a garden again. If you did that, you won't eat."

It is unlikely that the Doer government would have bought Versatile even if there were no strike underway at the time. The Manitoba NDP had long since lost its appetite for investing in private firms, especially given its experience in the 1970s when public ownership of Flyer, Saunders Aircraft and a host of smaller firms turned into political liabilities. Doer was not even a proponent of expanding the public sector (except in the area of health care), although one of his central campaign promises in the 1999 election was a commitment not to privatize Manitoba Hydro. Nor did his government follow the lead of Britain's ruling New Labour Party, which after coming to power in 1997 made public-private partnerships the centrepiece of what amounted to a strategy of privatization by stealth.

The Doer government was also far less generous with the private sector than was the Filmon government, which made over $100 million in loans to private business. The NDP had to write off the loans when it took office in 1999. As one observer of the provincial economy puts it, the government has been "tight with the business community in both senses of the word." When the owners of the New Flyer (the name that Flyer took on when it was sold to the private sector in the 1980s) bus firm and Motor Coach Industries came to the government looking for handouts during Doer's first term, the government was faced with a dilemma. Large numbers of unionized jobs were at risk (including CAW jobs at New Flyer) in industries that were profitable. New Flyer's financial problems were the result of growing too fast; it needed an injection of capital or its bankers would call in its loans. Motor Coach was looking at consolidating its operations, and threatened to leave Manitoba unless it got money from the government, concessions from the union, and tax breaks from the city. In the case of New Flyer, the government refused to provide loan guarantees, forcing the owners to sell to a company that was in a position to make the needed investments. The government provided secured loans that facilitated the deal and tied the company to the local economy. The province refused to provide Motor Coach with direct grants to keep it in the province. Instead, it made funds available on conditions that committed the company to training, maintaining local employment, expanding their facilities, and locating management and engineering in Manitoba. The deal, which did not go through without concessions from the union, was soured by the subsequent downturn in the North American travel market following the September 2001 terrorist attacks in the United States. Despite these reservations, in both cases the province was able to retain industrial employment at a limited cost.

But if the NDP proved in power to be more tightfisted than the Conservatives, the party has also sought to foster a tight relationship with the business community. Immediately after taking office the government hosted an economic summit. Later it decided to back off on a number of proposed labour law reforms, and it produced a notable lack of action on such issues as plant-closing legislation or anti-scab legislation. Still, in the future, workers who find themselves in the same fix as Local 2224 members will at least be able to use a recent NDP change to the labour code that allows them to force their employer into accepting binding arbitration after they have been on the picket line for sixty days. If nothing else, that kind of provision allows a union to lead an orderly retreat and protect its members' jobs. The British economist John Maynard Keynes noted that business confidence depends on nothing more firm than the easily spooked animal spirits of investors: taking over a business would certainly spook the horses and therefore was simply not on the NDP agenda.

A drive around the Versatile plant in the spring of 2004 underscored a basic reality: Versatile had not been saved, but scavenged. The main building was distinguished by a large sign announcing office space for lease. Those office workers who had not been laid off had been transferred to Buhler's offices in Transcona. The shipping building and part of its yard had been leased to a lumber company, and another "for lease" sign adorned the former parts building. Just after noon on a Monday the company parking lot had rows and rows of empty stalls. As Scott McLaren and I circled the plant, we looked for signs of life. Two huge tractors were turning desultory circles in a testing lot; elsewhere a tractor was being driven onto a truck trailer; and that was it. In the old days, McLaren told me, about fifty or sixty trucks would be lined up waiting to be unloaded on a Monday. "It would be go, go, go, unloading trucks. There would be forklifts moving material. And we would be producing over forty tractors a day. In that yard there would be fifteen or thirty trailers ready to be loaded, not one. Down here by the paint shop, these doors would be open, you would see traffic all along here." On our visit the plant seemed all but dead. In the fifteen minutes we spent driving around we never saw more than one worker.

The Versatile plant was still in business, but was no longer making the contribution that it once provided to the Manitoba economy. It now employed but a fraction of its previous workforce. Its development capacity had been scattered to the winds, and the new workers did not enjoy the wages and benefits gained by the old pre-strike workers. The future for those former Versatile workers and their families was one of uncertainty and, at best, diminished expectations. For a small province with a limited economic base, the changes at Versatile represent a significant loss. They are also bracing reminders of the dangers that arise when investment decisions that have an impact on the futures of hundreds or even thousands of people are made by private individuals on the basis of corporate profits.

The tractor industry has been undergoing a constant process of monopolization over the past hundred years. Numerous government investigations have concluded that the major tractor corporations were at times fixing prices and gouging farmers, but no serious efforts were made to curb this growing concentration. While the U.S. Department of Justice required New Holland to sell off its Versatile tractor lines, by allowing the Case New Holland merger to go ahead it gave its stamp of approval to what amounted to the end of competition in the tractor industry.

The best that Canadian politicians could do in this situation was grease the way for John Buhler to take over the Versatile plant, lobbying on his behalf with the U.S. Department of Justice and then giving him more money than he needed to buy the plant. From the outset, it seems, Buhler structured these deals to provide himself with the opportunity either to leave the country or at least make credible threats to that effect. Once the government bought him the plant, he proclaimed himself saviour and warned men who had spent their entire working lives building Versatile tractors that they would have to earn their job security from scratch. When Buhler threatened to relocate a company that had over the past thirty years supped long and deep at the public trough, the federal and provincial governments were all but powerless in their response.

This process by which corporations play communities and nations off against each other by threatening to move is a factor of globalization. Over the last thirty years politicians and corporate leaders have changed the rules of the economic game, making it easier for companies to shut down plants and move their operations to whatever place will give them the best deal. At the same time corporations have sought to reduce their responsibility to their workers, usually by contracting out component production to smaller non-unionized firms, in the process moving workers from a protected to a very competitive—and low-wage— labour market. These trends have made both workers and governments vulnerable to the sort of corporate blackmail that characterized Versa- tile's later years in Manitoba. While changes in technology provide corporations with the ability to shift production from one jurisdiction to another at a relatively low cost, the key changes have been political. To attract investment, governments have surrendered their rights to promote domestic industries. They have cut corporate taxes, weakened union bargaining rights, and reduced social benefits.

These political changes, unlike technological innovations, are reversible. In his social history of tractors in North America, Robert C. Williams concludes that throughout the twentieth century the increased use of tractors "expropriated rural wealth and showered it on urban corporations." But, he writes, it is not the tractor that is to blame. "In fact, tractors and other machinery are but scapegoats for a society that has never been able to address the unconscious centralization of economic power into ever fewer, but ever bigger, heedless corporations."[12] The development of a global economy need not, then, result in a race to the bottom. What we need instead is to establish some form of democratic control over the decisions that these ever-growing, ever-heedless corporations make. To use Canadian poet and politician Frank Scott's phrase, communities (both rural and urban) and workers will continue to be subject to turmoil, dislocation, and exploitation unless "power is brought to the pooling." Taking that step requires national economic policies that increase employment, trade policies that don't leave all decisions to the judgment of the market, and development policies that strengthen communities. This short list, though it might sound utopian, reflects a bare minimum for significant economic security. Corporations will not simply relinquish the tremendous powers and rights that they have acquired over the past thirty years; privilege and inequality never make concessions willingly. Any successful struggle to expand the bounds of democracy and equality will require sacrifice and solidarity.

The Versatile strike is a bracing reminder that these resources of hope are not as scarce as it might at first seem. During the darkest days of the Versatile strike, Scott McLaren used to buck up his fellow strikers by telling them that but for the efforts of ordinary men, evil triumphs. Despite their best efforts ordinary men and women may not always persevere, but without the sort of stubborn resistance and loyalty that the Versatile workers displayed, no progress is possible—besides which, what self-respecting person would have wanted to be on the other side?

Notes

2. VERSATILE TRACTORS

1. Jarrod Pakosh, *Versatile Tractors: A Farm Boy's Dream* (Erin, Ont: Boston Mills Press, 2003); Jennifer Bain, "Design Pioneer Made Equipment for Farmers, *The National Post* (Toronto), Feb. 23, 1999.
2. Ruben Bellan, *Winnipeg's First Century: An Economic History* (Winnipeg: Queenston House, 1978).
3. Grant MacEwan, *Power for Prairie Plows* (Saskatoon: Western Prairie Producer Books, 1979), 104.
4. Robert C. Williams, *Fordson, Farmall, and Poppin' Johnny: A History of the Farm Tractor and Its Impact on America* (Urbana: University of Illinois Press, 1987), 174.
5. Ibid.
6. Ibid., 104–105.
7. MacEwan, *Power for Prairie Plows*, 101.
8. Ibid..
9. Williams, *Fordson, Farmall, and Poppin' Johnny*, 112.
10. Sid Green, *Rise and Fall of a Political Animal: A Memoir* (Winnipeg: Great Plains Publications, 2003), 138–39.
11. Williams, *Fordson, Farmall, and Poppin' Johnny*, 115–16.
12. Jennifer Bain, "Design Pioneer Made Equipment for Farmers," *The National Post*, Feb. 23, 1999.
13. Harry L. Mardon, "Vancouver Conglomerate Buys Controlling Interest in Versatile," *Winnipeg Tribune*, Sept. 18, 1976; Harry L. Mardon, "Story behind the Versatile Sale to Cornat," *Winnipeg Tribune*, Sept. 24, 1976.
14. Pakosh, *Versatile Tractors*, 88.
15. Martin Cash, "Tractor Chief Avoided Brink, *Winnipeg Free Press*, Jan.10, 1996.
16. Catherine Gourley, "Peter Paul Saunders: Keeping Versatile," *Skyword*, June 1983; Nick Mitchell, "Specialization Brings Success Abroad for Versatile," *Manitoba Business*, August 1984.
17. "Versatile Sells Assets to Deere," *Winnipeg Free Press*, Dec. 11, 1985.
18. John Douglas, "Winnipeg Targeted as Tractor Capital," *Winnipeg Free Press*, Feb. 18, 1987; Geoffrey York, "Ford to Purchase Winnipeg Tractor Maker," *The Globe and Mail* (Toronto), Feb. 18, 1987; Donald Benham, "The Long Road Back," *Manitoba Business*, October 1987; *Canada Gazette*, Part 2, Vol. 121, no. 8 (1987), 1662.
19. Murray McNeill, "Versatile Reaps Global Recognition," *Winnipeg Free Press*, Jan. 3, 1990.
20. Aldo Santin, "New Layoffs, Closings Add to Versatile Plunge, *Winnipeg Free Press*, April 2, 1991.
21. Neal Asherson, "Under the Turin Cloud," *The Observer* (London), Nov. 19, 2000.
22. Alan Friedman, *Agnelli and the Network of Italian Power* (London: Harrap, 1988), 16.

23. Gail Edmondson et al., "Fiat: Running on Empty," *Business Week*, May 13, 2002.
24. Alan Friedman, "Fiat's 'Tough Guy' Chairman Is Found Guilty of Corruption," *International Herald Tribune*, April 10, 1997.
25. Ken Silverstein, "Ford and the Fuhrer," *The Nation*, Jan. 24, 2000.
26. Irving Bernstein, *The Lean Years: A History of the American Worker: 1920–1933* (Boston: Houghton Mifflin Company, 1972), 433–34.
27. John Douglas, "Fiat Promises More Jobs as Versatile Takeover OK'd," *Winnipeg Free Press*, April 19, 1992.
28. Aldo Santin, "Outlook Bleak at Versatile," *Winnipeg Free Press*, July 4, 1992; Martin Cash, "Versatile Plows Ahead," *Winnipeg Free Press*, April 29, 1993.
29. Martin Cash, "Canada's Only Tractor Maker Celebrates 10,000th Product," *Winnipeg Free Press*, June 18, 1996.
30. Gord Gooding, "Consistency and Reliability: New Holland's Versatile Farm Equipment Operations in New Holland," *Trade and Commerce Magazine* (supplement), 1998.

3. WHO BUILDS TRACTORS?

1. Quoted in Bryan Palmer and Gregory S. Kealey, *Dreaming of What Might Be: The Knights of Labor in Ontario 1880–1990* (Toronto: New Hogtown Press, 1987), 115.
2. Eugene Forsey, *Trade Unions in Canada, 1812–1902* (Toronto: University of Toronto Press, 1982), 147–48.
3. Gregory S. Kealey, *Toronto Workers Respond to Industrial Capitalism, 1867–1892* (Toronto: University of Toronto Press, 1980), 73–75.
4. David Montgomery, *The Fall of the House of Labour: The Workplace, the State, and American Labour Activism, 1865–1925* (Cambridge, Cambridge University Press, 1987), 269–70.
5. Jeremy Brecher, *Strike! The True History of Mass Insurgence in America from 1877 to the Present* (Boston: South End Press, 1972), 117–18.
6. Irving Bernstein, *The Lean Years: A History of the American Worker, 1920–1933* (Boston: Houghton Mifflin Company, 1972), 156.
7. James Green, *The World of the Worker* (New York: Hill and Wang, 1980), 103.
8. Richard Edwards, *Contested Terrain: The Transformation of the Workplace in the Twentieth Century* (New York: Basic Books, 1979), 108.
9. Bruce Scott, "'A Place in the Sun': The Industrial Council at Massey Harris, 1919–1929," *Labour/Le Travailleur*, vol. 1 (1976), 176–77.
10. Ibid., 185.
11. *The Toronto Daily Star*, April 9, 1937.
12. Harvey Klehr, *The Heyday of American Communism: The Depression Decade* (New York: Basic Books, 1984), 237; Melvyn Dubofsky, *The State and Labor in Modern America* (Chapel Hill: University of North Carolina Press, 1994), 172.
13. Toni Gilpin, "Labor's Last Stand," *Chicago History*, vol.18, issue 1 (1989), 47.
14. Toni Gilpin, "Left by Themselves: A History of the United Farm Equipment and Metal Workers Union, 1938–1955," Ph.D. thesis, Yale University, New Haven, Conn., 1992.
15. Sam Gindin, *The Canadian Auto Workers: The Birth and Transformation of a Union* (Toronto: James Lorimer and Company, 1995), 217.

4. BUILDING A LOCAL: 1985–2000

1. David Roberts, "Unique Deal Covers Legal Bills," *Winnipeg Free Press*, Oct. 31, 1988.
2. Tom Rankin, *New Forms of Work Organization: The Challenge for North American Unions* (Toronto : University of Toronto Press, 1990).
3. Local 2224, CAW, "Message from Your Local Union," Winnipeg, Sept. 25, 1998.
4. "Strike over at Versatile," *Winnipeg Free Press*, Nov. 9, 1994.

5. THE MERGER AND ITS FALLOUT: 1999–2000

1. Alby Gallun, "Case-New Holland Reaps Global Economy," *The Business Journal of Milwaukee*, May 24, 1999.
2. J.I. Case Corporation, news release, May 17, 1999.
3. Buzz Hargrove to John Manley and Gary Filmon, May 20, 1999.
4. Buzz Hargrove to Gary Filmon, May 19, 1999.
5. Martin Cash, "Merger Talk Creating Uncertainty at Versatile," *Winnipeg Free Press*, July 8, 1999.
6. Martin Cash, "Versatile Tractor Plant up for Sale," *Winnipeg Free Press*, Nov. 5, 1999.
7. Neil Versel and Linda Tamas, "CNH: Potential Buyer Interest Reportedly Made for Winnipeg Tractor Plant, *Starks News Service*, Nov. 17, 1999.
8. Judy Waytiuk, "Buhler Logic: A Bizarre Business Approach, but It Works, *Commerce & Industry*, September 1998.
9. Michael Decter, *Michael Decter's Million Dollar Strategy: Building Your Own Retirement Fund in Just Thirty Minutes a Day* (Toronto: Stoddart, 1998), 111–13.
10. Martin Cash, "Farm Equipment Magnate Usually Holds Winning Hand," *Winnipeg Free Press*, June 26, 2000.
11. Martin Cash, "Buhler Wants Second Crack at Buying Versatile Plant," *Winnipeg Free Press*, Nov. 20, 1999.
12. Cash, "Farm Equipment Magnate Usually Holds Winning Hand."
13. Paul Samyn, "Versatile Closure Even More Costly?" *Winnipeg Free Press*, Nov. 19, 1999.
14. Len Rausch and Scott McLaren to Gary Doer, Dec. 15, 1999.
15. CAW, news release, Dec. 9, 1999.
16. Len Rausch and Scott McLaren to all CAW Local Presidents and Chairpersons, February 2000.
17. David Morgan to Dale Paterson, Aug. 27, 1999.
18. Associated Press, "Versatile's Plant in City Closing Doors," *Winnipeg Free Press*, Feb. 2, 2000.
19. Martin Cash, "U.S. May Kill Versatile Sale," *Winnipeg Free Press*, April 19, 2000.
20. Murray McNeill, "Buhler Won't Let Factory Bid Die without a Fight," *Winnipeg Free Press*, April 28, 2000.
21. "Regulations Amending the Ford New Holland, IC Loan Regulation PC 2000-1035," June 12, 2000, *Canada Gazette*, part II, vol.134, no. 14 (July 2000), 1715.
22. Ibid.
23. Buhler Industries, news release, Winnipeg, June 16, 2000.

24. <http://www.buhler.com/buhler/news200009-27b.htm>.
25. Cash, "Farm Equipment Magnate Usually Holds Winning Hand."
26. Decter, *Michael Decter's Million Dollar Strategy*, 13.

6. NEGOTIATIONS: SUMMER TO FALL 2000

1. Martin Cash, "Unions Shouldn't Bank on Buhler's Hardship," *Winnipeg Free Press*, Feb. 1, 2001.
2. Dale Paterson to David Morgan, July 6, 2000.
3. Martin Cash, "Salaried Versatile Staff Offered Severance, Jobs," *Winnipeg Free Press*, July 13, 2000.
4. Martin Cash, "Company High $100 Million a Year Mark This Month," *Winnipeg Free Press*, Sept. 27, 2000.
5. United Auto Workers, "UAW on Plant Closings: CNH Global Puts Profits Ahead of Workers," UAW website <http://www.uaw.org/solidarity/00/1000/union06.html> (accessed April 8, 2004).
6. Craig McEwen, "Fargo Case-NH May Grow," *Fargo-Moorehead Forum*, Oct. 31, 2000.
7. Rich Rovito, "Some CNH Jobs Saved by 11th-Hour Negotiations," *The Business Journal of Milwaukee*, Nov. 6, 2000; "CNH to Create Tractor Assembly Plant in Racine," *The Business Journal of Milwaukee*, Nov. 17, 2000.

7. THE STRIKE BEGINS: NOVEMBER TO DECEMBER 2000

1. Helen Bergen to Dale Paterson, Nov. 8, 2000.
2. Martin Cash, "Tractor Factory Workers on Strike," *Winnipeg Free Press*, Nov. 7, 2000.
3. Manitoba, *Manitoba Labour Relations Act* <http://web2.gov.mb.ca/laws/statutes/ccsm/l010e.php> (accessed April 9, 2004).
4. Helen Bergen to Scott McLaren, Dec. 11, 2000.
5. Bud Robertson, "Buhler Offers $500,000 for Transcona Health Unit," *Winnipeg Free Press*, Dec. 22, 2000.

8. THE THREAT OF PLANT CLOSURE: JANUARY TO FEBRUARY

1. Craig Engel to Becky Barrett, Jan. 15, 2001.
2. Martin Cash, "Buhler May Bypass Union to Build Tractors," *Winnipeg Free Press*, Jan. 19, 2001.
3. Wendy Stephenson, "Buhler about to Bolt," *Winnipeg Sun*, Jan. 23, 2001.
4. Jonathan Knutson, "W. Fargo May Land Tractor Plant," *Fargo-Moorehead Forum*, Jan. 18, 2001.
5. Stephenson, "Buhler about to Bolt."
6. MaryAnn Mihychuk to Brian Tobin, Jan. 25, 2001.
7. Martin Cash, "Buhler's Fargo Plans Called 'Scare Tactic,'" *Winnipeg Free Press*, Jan. 18, 2001.
8. Helen Fallding, "NDP Appoints Mediator, to Help End Buhler Strike," *Winnipeg Free Press*, Jan. 25, 2001.

9. Helen Fallding, "Binding Arbitration Urged in Buhler Strike," *Winnipeg Free Press*, Feb. 15, 2001.
10. Craig Engel to Wally Fox-Decent, Feb. 16, 2001.
11. Martin Cash, "Mediator Can't End Strike at Buhler," *Winnipeg Free Press*, Feb. 17, 2001.
12. Tom Brodbeck, "Factory Is Moving and It's All Over," *Winnipeg Sun*, Feb. 17, 2001.
13. Cathy Pitcher, "Politicians Ignore Tractor Plant Fate," *Winnipeg Free Press,* Jan. 30, 2001.
14. Canada, House of Commons, *Hansard*, Feb. 27, 2001.
15. Paul Moist to all NDP MLAs, Feb. 23, 2001.
16. Cary Castagna, "Fed Loan to Buhler Blasted," *Winnipeg Sun*, Feb. 23, 2001.
17. Local 2224, CAW, "Application for an Unfair Labour Practice between National Automobile, Aerospace, Transportation, and General Workers Union of Canada and Local 2224 and Buhler Industries," Winnipeg, Feb. 23, 2001.
18. Martin Cash, "Union Skit Has Buhler Fleeing with Tax Money," *Winnipeg Free Press*, Feb. 24, 2001.
19. Martin Cash, "Unions Shouldn't Bank on Buhler's Hardship," *Winnipeg Free Press*, Feb. 1, 2001.
20. "Failure at Versatile," *Winnipeg Free Press*, March 1, 2001.

9. Cowboy Capitalists and Labour-Friendly Governments: A Long March

1. Green, *Rise and Fall of a Political Animal*, 140.
2. Sean O'Connor, "Striking Buhler Staff Protest $32-M Loan," *Winnipeg Free Press*, March 2, 2001.
3. Alexandra Paul, "CAW's Buzz Hargrove Urges Nationalization of Versatile," *Winnipeg Free Press*, March 3, 2001.
4. Leah Hendry, "Tractor Plant Takeover Urged," *Winnipeg Free Press*, March 4, 2003.
5. Tim Brodbeck, "Province Won't Buy Tractor Firm," *Winnipeg Sun*, March 6, 2001.
6. Tim Brodbeck, "Hargrove to NDP: Buzz Off," *Winnipeg Sun,* March 7, 2001; Martin Cash, "Bad Time, Bad Call by Union at Versatile," *Winnipeg Free Press*, March 8, 2001.
7. David Kuxhaus, "Buhler Defends Plan to Move Tractor Plant," *Winnipeg Free Press*, March 8, 2001.
8. Leah Hendry, "Union Increases Effort to Keep Buhler Jobs Here," *Winnipeg Free Press*, March 18, 2001.
9. CAW, "Discussion Points on the Future of the Versatile-Buhler Tractor Facility," Winnipeg, n.d.
10. Cary Castagna, "Buhler Laughs off Union Bid," *Winnipeg Sun*, March 18, 2001.
11. Jim Stanford to Craig Engel, March 20, 2001.
12. Craig Engel to Jim Stanford, March 30, 2001.
13. Manitoba NDP, "Another Winnipeg Plant Closure," press release, Winnipeg, Feb. 6, 1990; "Party Atmosphere Belies Mood of Buhler Workers," *Winnipeg Free Press*, April 11, 2001.
14. Jim Silver, "Fighting Plant Closures," in *Hard Bargains: The Manitoba Labour*

Movement Confronts the 1990s, ed. Errol Black and Jim Silver (Winnipeg: Manitoba Labour Education Centre, 1991).

15. Ken Georgetti to Brian Tobin, April 2, 2001.
16. New Democratic Party, "NDP Labour Critic Pat Martin Demands Repayment of Buhler Loans," news release, Ottawa, April 11, 2001.
17. "Union Testifies Buhler 'Taunted,'" *Winnipeg Sun*, March 20, 2001; "CAW Seeking \$5 Million from Tractor Manufacturer, CBC-TV, Winnipeg, March 19, 2001.
18. Hemi Mitic to Craig Engel, March 26, 2001.
19. Craig Engel to Dale Paterson, March 27, 2001.
20. "Buhler Locks out Returning Workers," CBC-TV, Winnipeg, March 27, 2001.

10. From Lockout to Severance: April to August 2001

1. Tracey Epp to Manitoba Labour Board, April 19, 2001.
2. Tracey Epp to Manitoba Labour Board, April 19, 2001.
3. Martin Cash, "Buhler Lawyer Fights Union Charges," *Winnipeg Free Press*, April 18, 2001.
4. Craig Engel, submission to Manitoba Labour Board, April 25, 2001.
5. Martin Cash, "Feds out on Limb if Tractor Plant Folds," *Winnipeg Free Press*, May 5, 2002.
6. "Hearing Told Company, Not Union, Lost Tractor Contract, CBC News, Winnipeg, May 8, 2001.
7. Martin Cash, "Buhler Rules out Tractors at Plant," *Winnipeg Free Press*, May 9, 2001.
8. Martin Cash, "Buhler Quizzed on Tractor Deal Failure," *Winnipeg Free Press*, May 15, 2001.
9. Martin Cash, "Wpg. Plant Destined to Go: Expert," *Winnipeg Free Press*, May 17, 2001.
10. Martin Cash, "Weird Things Happening at Labour Board's Versatile Hearing," *Winnipeg Free Press*, May 10, 2001.
11. Martin Cash, "Wide-Ranging Implications Expected from Buhler Ruling," *Winnipeg Free Press*, May 19, 2001.
12. "Buhler 'Devastated' over Labour Board Ruling," CBC-TV, Winnipeg, June 7, 2002.
13. Brendan O'Hallarn, "No More Manitoba Job Creation: Businessman," *Winnipeg Sun*, June 8, 2001.
14. Martin Cash, "Labour Board Lashes Buhler," June 8, 2001; Martin Cash, "Buhler, CAW Butt Heads Anew," *Winnipeg Free Press*, June 20, 2001.
15. Geoff Kirbyson, "Union Seeks \$18 Million in Damages from Buhler," *Winnipeg Free Press*, June 26, 2001.
16. "Buhler to Pay Union up to \$6 million," CBC news, Winnipeg, July 19, 2001.
17. Wendy Stephenson, "Buhler Told to Pay \$6 Million," *Winnipeg Sun*, July 19, 2001.
18. Geoff Kirbyson, "Buhler Told to Pay Up," *Winnipeg Free Press*, July 19, 2001.
19. "Buhler Plant Losing Jobs: CEO," CBC-TV news, Winnipeg, July 23, 2001.
20. Martin Cash, "Buhler Plans to Appeal Labour Board Ruling," *Winnipeg Free Press*, July 24, 2001.
21. Manitoba Labour Board, "Decision," case no. 220/01//LRA, Winnipeg, July 30,

2001, 12.
22. Ibid.
23. Ibid, 16.
24. Ibid., 17–18.
25. Ibid., 19.
26. "Bad Faith at Versatile," *Winnipeg Free Press*, July 19, 2001.
27. Paul McKie, "A Bitter End at Buhler," *Winnipeg Free Press*, Aug. 14, 2001.
28. Martin Cash, "When Settling Just Makes Sense," *Winnipeg Free Press*, Aug. 30, 2001.

11. BETWEEN THE DEVIL AND THE DEEP BLUE SEA

1. Buhler Industries, "Buhler Settles with Canadian Auto Workers," press release, Winnipeg, Aug. 14, 2001.
2. David Parkinson, "Buhler Ends Dispute by Paying to Rid Itself of Union Workers," *The Globe and Mail*, Aug. 15, 2001; Murray McNeill, "Buhler's Future Remains up in the Air, *Winnipeg Free Press*, Aug. 15, 2001; Wendy Stephenson, "Buhler Licks Wounds," *Winnipeg Sun*, Aug. 15, 2001.
3. Harry Siemens, "Buhler Success Continues into First Full Year," *Manitoba Co-operator*, Jan. 22, 2003.
4. Martin Cash, "Buhler Bullish Despite Drop in Sales, Profit," *Winnipeg Free Press*, April 22, 2003.
5. Martin Cash, "Buhler Industries 'Very Pleased with Results,'" *Winnipeg Free Press*, Dec. 13, 2003.
6. Neil Scott, "Maverick Slams Unions, Politicians," *The Leader Post* (Regina), June 19, 2003.
7. Martin Cash, "Buhler's Third Quarter Results on Target," *Winnipeg Free Press*, July 18, 2003.
8. Rich Rovito, "CNH Says Case, New Holland Tractors Will Harvest Profits," *The Business Journal of Greater Milwaukee*, June 28, 2002.
9. Mark Milner, "Image of Industrial Italy Shrinks," *The Guardian* (London), June 27, 2003.
10. "Farm Equipment Maker Cuts Profit," *The New York Times*, Oct. 4, 2003.
11. William Ryberg, "Several Iowa Labor Contracts on Table," *Des Moines Register*, Aug. 31, 2003.
12. Williams, *Fordson, Farmall, and Poppin' Johnny*, 186.